FANTASTIC FACTOIDS FOR THE INSANELY CURIOUS

A COLLECTION OF STRANGE, BUT TRUE, AND
OFTEN UNHEARD-OF FACTOIDS THAT WILL
BLOW YOUR MIND

M. PATRICK SAUER

TABLE OF CONTENTS

INTRODUCTION

Welcome to Fantastic Factoids for the Insanely Curious: a collection of strange, but true, and often unheard-of facts that will blow your mind. Contained within this book are some of the most unusual, strangest, and sometimes completely absurd facts that you've likely never heard. There are 41 themes and over 150 thought provoking and captivating illustrations designed to get the reader's attention and stimulate conversation.

Each chapter of this book will expose the reader to a new set of facts. Whether you want to read about civilizations, empires, historical figures, inventions, animals, legends, folklore, or space you'll find it, and much more inside.

Fantastic Factoids was designed for families as a source of entertainment and education and can be enjoyed by readers from 10 to 100 years old. Unlike other books of this genre, Fantastic Factoids has selected as its chapter topics subject matter that will surely peak the readers interest and will build on subjects that have likely been taught or will soon be learned in school. Simply put, our goal in choosing factoids was to encourage further reading and foster a desire for the reader to delve deeper into the topics with some independent research.

We've been told that this book is like going on a different intellectual journey every time you pick it up. Whether you read it at home in the living room, bedroom, or bathroom this book will make for an ideal companion that is sure to keep you entertained, engaged, and curious. Share it with your friends, family, teachers, and classmates. Take it to the beach, the pool, on long road trips or on an airplane. Whichever way you choose to enjoy our book we guarantee for certain one thing, and one thing only. You will get smarter having read it!

Ancient Civilizations

The Sumerians' Beer Rations: In ancient Sumeria, beer was a staple of daily life, so much so that workers received beer rations as part of their wages. This brew, known as "kash," was considered nutritious and safer to drink than water due to the fermentation process, making it essential for sustaining the labor force.

The Egyptians' Cat Cult

Ancient Egyptians held cats in the highest esteem, considering them divine beings worthy of adoration and reverence. The goddess Bastet, depicted as a lioness or a woman with the head of a lioness, embodied the protective and nurturing qualities associated with felines. Cats were not only cherished as beloved companions but also revered for their role in safeguarding homes and granaries from rodents and pests, contributing to the prosperity of Egyptian society. In temples dedicated to Bastet, lavish offerings were presented to honor these revered creatures, and mummified cats were buried alongside their human counterparts to ensure safe passage to the afterlife. This profound reverence for cats underscores the deep spiritual connection between the ancient Egyptians and the enigmatic feline companions who shared their homes and hearts.

The Chinese Oracle Bones: During the Shang Dynasty in ancient China, divination rituals involved the use of oracle bones, typically ox scapulae or turtle plastrons, inscribed with questions to the gods. After heating the bones, cracks would form, and priests interpreted these patterns as divine messages, offering guidance on matters of state, agriculture, and warfare.

The Olmec Rubber Ball Game: The Olmec civilization of ancient Mesoamerica played a ball game using a solid rubber ball, often as part of religious ceremonies. Players would bounce the ball off their hips, aiming to pass it through stone hoops mounted on walls, with the game symbolizing cosmic battles and the cycle of life and death.

The Minoans' Bull-Leaping Rituals: The Minoan civilization of ancient Crete practiced a dangerous sport known as bull-leaping, where athletes vaulted over charging bulls in acrobatic displays of agility and bravery. This ritual, depicted in Minoan frescoes, likely had religious significance, symbolizing the triumph of humanity over nature.

The Nazca Lines' Gigantic Geoglyphs: The Nazca Lines, located in the Peruvian desert, consist of enormous geoglyphs depicting animals, plants, and geometric shapes, created by the Nazca culture over 2,000 years ago. The purpose of these massive earthworks remains a subject of debate among archaeologists, with theories ranging from religious rituals to astronomical calendars.

The Harappans' Standardized Weights: The ancient Indus Valley civilization utilized standardized weights made of materials such as steatite or bronze for trade and commerce. These weights were intricately carved and ranged from tiny units for measuring precious metals to larger units for commodities like grain and textiles, indicating a sophisticated system of economic regulation.

The Etruscans' Wine-Drinking Parties: Etruscan banquets were lavish affairs characterized by copious amounts of wine, entertainment, and elaborate cuisine. Guests reclined on couches while musicians played, and dancers entertained, reflecting the Etruscans' appreciation for hedonistic pleasures and socializing.

The Sumerians' Writing System:

The Sumerians of ancient Mesopotamia developed one of the earliest known writing systems, known as cuneiform, around 3200 BCE. Originally pictographic, cuneiform evolved into a complex script consisting of wedge-shaped characters impressed onto clay tablets, used for recording administrative, economic, and literary texts.

The Moche Sacrificial Ceremonies: The Moche civilization of ancient Peru conducted elaborate sacrificial ceremonies to appease their gods and ensure agricultural fertility. These rituals often involved the ritualistic killing of captives or members of the elite, with their blood believed to nourish the earth and sustain the community.

The Nabateans' Water Conservation Methods: The ancient Nabateans, who inhabited the desert region of Petra in present-day Jordan, developed innovative water conservation techniques to overcome arid conditions. They constructed elaborate systems of dams, cisterns, and terraces to collect and store rainwater, enabling agriculture and supporting their thriving city.

The Carthaginian Child Sacrifice: Carthaginians practiced ritual child sacrifice as offerings to their gods, particularly during times of crisis or war. Infants or young children were cremated alive in the arms of large bronze statues of the god Baal, with the gruesome practice documented by ancient historians and archaeologists.

The Hittite Treaty Tablets: The Hittites of ancient Anatolia were among the first civilizations to develop written treaties, which were inscribed on clay tablets. These treaties, such as the Treaty of Kadesh between the Hittites and Egyptians, established diplomatic agreements and delineated borders, showcasing the Hittites' diplomatic prowess and administrative sophistication.

The Assyrian Library at Nineveh: The ancient Assyrians built one of the world's first libraries at Nineveh, containing thousands of clay tablets inscribed with cuneiform script. This vast collection included administrative records, literary texts, and scientific treatises, providing valuable insights into Assyrian culture, history, and knowledge.

The Parthian Cataphracts: The Parthians of ancient Iran fielded heavily armored cavalry known as cataphracts, who played a crucial role in their military campaigns. These elite warriors wore scale armor and wielded lances and bows from atop their armored horses, striking fear into the hearts of their enemies with their formidable charges.

The Zapotec Ballcourt Complexes

The Zapotec civilization, renowned for its advanced understanding of architecture and urban planning, left behind impressive ballcourt complexes that served as focal points for communal activities. These ballcourts were not merely arenas for sporting events but also sacred spaces imbued with spiritual significance. The Mesoamerican ballgame, played within these complexes, held deep religious and cosmological meanings for the Zapotec people, symbolizing cosmic battles, fertility rites, and the cyclical nature of life and death. The game's ritualistic nature was often intertwined with religious ceremonies, reflecting the Zapotec's profound connection to their gods and the natural world.

The Phoenician Purple Dye: Phoenicians were renowned for their production of purple dye, extracted from the glands of marine mollusks found in the eastern Mediterranean. Known as "Tyrian purple," this rare and expensive dye was highly prized by royalty and nobility in ancient times, symbolizing wealth, status, and power.

The Indus Valley's Advanced Sanitation: The ancient Indus Valley civilization, dating back over 4,000 years, had remarkably advanced sanitation systems. Their cities featured sophisticated drainage networks, public baths, and even flush toilets in some homes, demonstrating a remarkable understanding of urban planning and hygiene.

The Mayans' Tooth Decoration: The Mayans' practice of dental modification, known as "teeth filing," was not only a form of body modification but also a symbol of social status and beauty within their society. By drilling holes in their teeth and embedding precious stones like jade or obsidian, the Mayan elite demonstrated their wealth and elevated position in the community. Additionally, these dental decorations were believed to have spiritual significance, possibly serving as markers of identity or protection against malevolent forces in the afterlife. Despite its painful and potentially harmful nature, teeth filing persisted as a cultural tradition among the Mayan aristocracy, showcasing the importance of physical adornment and symbolism in their civilization.

The Aksumite Obelisks: The Aksumite civilization of ancient Ethiopia erected massive obelisks carved from single pieces of granite, some reaching heights of over 100 feet. These monumental structures served as royal tombs, markers of royal power, and symbols of Aksumite civilization, showcasing their architectural and engineering prowess.

The Renaissance Era

Sword Fighting Academies: During the Renaissance, sword fighting became a popular pastime among the European elite, leading to the establishment of specialized academies where nobles and gentlemen could learn the art of fencing and dueling. These academies not only taught practical combat skills but also emphasized the importance of honor, chivalry, and social etiquette in personal combat.

Poison Detection Tests: During the Renaissance, poison became a favored method of assassination. In response to this threat, rulers and nobles developed poison detection tests. Suspects would be administered a small dose of the suspected poison, often in the presence of witnesses, and then closely monitored for signs of poisoning. These tests ranged from ingesting small amounts of the substance to applying it to the skin or inhaling its fumes. However, the reliability and accuracy of these tests were questionable. Despite their limitations, poison detection tests were seen as a means of deterring would-be assassins and maintaining order in the volatile political landscape of the Renaissance.

Fashionable Codpieces: Codpieces, exaggerated pouches or coverings worn over the groin, became fashionable among European men during the Renaissance, serving both decorative and practical purposes. While initially designed to provide modesty and support for the male anatomy, codpieces evolved into elaborate and often exaggerated fashion statements, with some adorned with jewels, embroidery, or even hidden compartments.

Horticultural Oddities: Renaissance gardens were not only spaces of beauty and contemplation but also served as showcases for botanical curiosities and horticultural oddities. Wealthy patrons would commission elaborate gardens featuring exotic plants, rare flowers, and unusual fruits, showcasing their wealth, taste, and knowledge of the natural world.

Witchcraft Panics

The Renaissance saw a rise in witchcraft panics and persecutions, fueled by superstition, religious fervor, and fear of the supernatural. Suspected witches, often women accused of practicing dark magic or consorting with the devil, faced torture, imprisonment, and execution, as authorities sought to eradicate perceived threats to the social order and Christian faith. The infamous witch trials, such as those in Salem, Massachusetts, and the European witch hunts, resulted in the deaths of thousands of innocent individuals, highlighting the widespread hysteria and paranoia surrounding accusations of witchcraft during this period. Despite the Enlightenment's emphasis on reason and scientific inquiry, the fear of witches persisted, reflecting deep-seated anxieties about the unknown and the perceived dangers posed by marginalized members of society.

Memento Mori Art: Memento mori, Latin for "remember death," was a popular theme in Renaissance art, reminding viewers of the inevitability of death and the transient nature of life. Paintings, sculptures, and decorative objects featuring skulls, hourglasses, and other symbols of mortality served as sobering reminders to contemplate the fleeting nature of earthly existence and prepare for the afterlife.

Physiognomy: Physiognomy, the pseudoscientific practice of judging a person's character or personality based on their facial features, was widely believed and practiced during the Renaissance. Artists, scholars, and even rulers consulted physiognomists to assess a person's moral virtues, intelligence, and temperament, leading to widespread prejudice and discrimination based on superficial appearances.

Gastronomic Experiments: Renaissance banquets were elaborate affairs, featuring exotic delicacies, elaborate table settings, and theatrical entertainment. Chefs and gastronomes experimented with new ingredients, flavors, and cooking techniques, creating culinary delights such as sugar sculptures, edible works of art, and extravagant feasts designed to impress and delight their noble patrons.

Artificial Foreskins: In an age of religious fervor and social conformity, circumcision was considered a mark of Jewish identity and was often performed on male infants shortly after birth. However, some Renaissance men sought to reverse or conceal their circumcision using artificial foreskins made from animal skin, leather, or other materials, reflecting cultural anxieties and personal insecurities about masculinity and sexual identity.

Fasting Saints: Fasting was a common religious practice during the Renaissance, with many devout Christians, particularly monks, nuns, and ascetics, undertaking prolonged fasts as acts of piety and self-discipline. Some saints were renowned for their extreme fasting habits, going weeks or even months without food or water, as they sought to emulate the suffering of Christ and achieve spiritual enlightenment through self-denial.

Bloodletting Therapy: Despite its dubious efficacy and potential dangers, bloodletting remained a popular medical treatment during the Renaissance, based on the ancient theory of balancing the body's humors. Physicians and barber-surgeons used various methods to withdraw blood from patients, including leeches, lancets, and cupping, in the belief that it would purify the blood and restore health.

Bathing Prejudices: Contrary to modern hygiene practices, bathing was often discouraged or viewed with suspicion during the Renaissance, particularly in northern Europe, where it was associated with decadence, immorality, and disease. Many believed that bathing opened the pores of the skin to miasmas, or harmful vapors, leading to illness and infection, and preferred to maintain personal hygiene through perfumes, powders, and changing undergarments.

Exotic Pet Ownership: Renaissance nobles and royalty delighted in the ownership of exotic pets, importing rare and unusual animals from distant lands to showcase their wealth and status. Menageries and private collections featured creatures such as lions, elephants, monkeys, and parrots, serving as symbols of power, prestige, and cultural sophistication.

Animal Trials: In a bizarre twist of justice, animals were sometimes brought to trial and subjected to legal proceedings during the Renaissance, particularly in cases of alleged criminal behavior or damage to property. These "animal trials" often involved formal court proceedings, legal representation for the accused animal, and sentences ranging from banishment to death, reflecting the superstitious beliefs and anthropomorphic views of the time.

Lunar Calendars

During the Renaissance, lunar calendars played a crucial role in various aspects of society, ranging from religious observances to agricultural planning. Monks and scholars meticulously studied and recorded the phases of the moon and other celestial events, recognizing their significance in marking time and guiding human activities. Lunar cycles were particularly important for determining the dates of religious festivals and observances, as many Christian holidays were tied to the lunar calendar. Additionally, farmers relied on lunar phases to schedule planting, harvesting, and other agricultural tasks, recognizing the influence of the moon on tides, moisture levels, and plant growth. Furthermore, sailors used lunar observations to navigate the seas, relying on the moon's position in the night sky to determine their location and chart their course. Thus, lunar calendars served as essential tools for organizing and coordinating human endeavors, reflecting Renaissance society's deep reverence for the natural world and its rhythms.

Alchemy and Artistry: Renaissance artists often incorporated alchemical symbolism into their works, exploring the transformative processes of creation, and transmutation. Paintings, sculptures, and decorative objects featured alchemical symbols, allegorical figures, and esoteric imagery, inviting viewers to contemplate the mysteries of nature, spirituality, and the human soul.

Apotropaic Symbols: Apotropaic symbols, or symbols believed to ward off evil and protect against harm, were commonly used during the Renaissance to safeguard homes, churches, and individuals from malevolent forces. These symbols, including charms and talismans, were often incorporated into architectural elements, decorative objects, and religious artifacts, reflecting belief in the supernatural and the power of symbolism.

The Cult of the Beautiful Nose: In Italy, the nose was considered a symbol of beauty, intelligence, and social status, leading to a fascination with nasal aesthetics. Wealthy patrons, artists, and surgeons sought to enhance nasal features through cosmetic surgery, prosthetic devices, and elaborate hairstyles, reflecting cultural ideals of physical perfection and social conformity.

Hair Loss Remedies: With baldness considered undesirable during the Renaissance, various remedies were devised to combat hair loss and promote hair growth. These included concoctions made from animal fat, herbs, and urine, as well as bizarre practices like wearing hats made from the fur of animals or rubbing the scalp with nettles.

Alchemy and Astrology: Despite the advancements in science during the Renaissance, belief in alchemy and astrology remained widespread, with many intellectuals and scholars practicing these pseudoscientific disciplines alongside their legitimate studies. Alchemists sought to transmute base metals into gold and discover the elixir of life, while astrologers attempted to predict the future and understand the influence of celestial bodies on human affairs.

The Age of Enlightenment

The Great Cat Massacre: The incident of the Great Cat Massacre in 1730s France was a bizarre yet symbolic protest by apprentice printers against their oppressive working conditions. Inspired by Enlightenment ideals, particularly satire and reason, the workers staged a mock trial and execution of cats, which they associated with their abusive masters. This unusual act highlights the intersection of social discontent, cultural symbolism, and emerging Enlightenment thought during the period.

The Caliph of Cologne: The hoax surrounding the imaginary "Caliph of Cologne" in Enlightenment-era Germany underscores the power of rumor and imagination in shaping public perception. Despite lacking any factual basis, the prank captivated the citizens of Cologne, leading to extravagant preparations and excitement for the fictitious visit. This episode reflects the era's thirst for novelty, curiosity about distant cultures, and susceptibility to deception in an age of expanding global connections.

The Decline of Hats in Enlightenment England: The waning popularity of elaborate headgear in Enlightenment-era England reflects changing social norms and values. As Enlightenment ideals of reason and rationality gained prominence, ostentatious displays of wealth and status, such as extravagant wigs and hats, fell out of fashion. This cultural shift symbolizes the era's rejection of traditional hierarchies and its embrace of simplicity and practicality.

The Invention of the 'Philosopher's Hat': The concept of the "philosopher's hat," a wide-brimmed headpiece intended to shield the wearer's eyes from the glare of excessive knowledge, symbolizes the Enlightenment's pursuit of wisdom and enlightenment. While purely symbolic, the hat served as a visual representation of the philosopher's commitment to intellectual inquiry and pursuit of truth, embodying the era's ethos of reason and rationality.

The Enlightenment's 'Turban Fad'

The wearing of turbans among intellectuals and aristocrats in Enlightenment-era Europe reflects the era's fascination with Orientalism and exotic cultures. Individuals sought an image of cosmopolitanism and sophistication, influenced by their encounters with Eastern philosophies and travel narratives.

Voltaire's Obsession with Coffee Enemas: Voltaire's unconventional health practices, including his fondness for coffee enemas, reveal the era's preoccupation with bodily health and longevity. Despite lacking scientific validity, Voltaire's belief in the rejuvenating effects of coffee enemas reflects the Enlightenment's emphasis on empirical observation and experimentation. His eccentric habits underscore the intersection of Enlightenment ideals with personal quirks and beliefs.

The Philosophical Society of Brunch: The establishment of the "Philosophical Society of Brunch" as a forum for intellectual discussion underscores the informal and convivial nature of Enlightenment-era salons. By gathering over brunch, members of this society sought to engage in free-flowing conversation and exchange ideas in a relaxed setting. This informal approach to intellectual inquiry reflects the era's emphasis on sociability and camaraderie among intellectuals.

The Illuminati's 'Blue Sun' Ceremony

The Bavarian Illuminati's alleged ritual known as the "Blue Sun" ceremony represents the convergence of Enlightenment ideals with esoteric symbolism and secrecy. The exact nature of the ceremony remains a mystery. Conspiracy theories suggest that it involved mystical practices and occult rituals. This fascination with secret societies and hidden knowledge reflects the era's complex interplay between rationalism and mysticism.

The Quest for 'Philosophical Shoes': Enlightenment thinkers speculated about the possibility of designing "philosophical shoes" that would enhance the wearer's intellectual faculties and promote a more enlightened posture and gait. While such footwear was never realized, the idea reflects the era's belief in the potential for material objects to influence mental states and behavior, blurring the boundaries between science, philosophy, and fashion.

The Debate over 'Enlightened Despotism': Enlightenment philosophers engaged in debates over the concept of "enlightened despotism," which proposed that absolute monarchs could rule with enlightened principles and promote social progress. This controversial idea sparked heated discussions about the balance between authority and reform in governance, challenging traditional notions of sovereignty and power.

The Royal Society's Quest for a Language of Birds: The Royal Society's sponsorship of experiments to decipher a potential "language of birds" exemplifies the era's curiosity about the natural world and its belief in the universality of communication. By studying avian vocalizations and behavior, Enlightenment-era naturalists sought to uncover underlying patterns and meanings in bird language. Despite the lack of scientific basis for such endeavors, they reflect the era's fascination with uncovering hidden truths in nature.

The 'Satanic Verses' Controversy: European scholars in the Enlightenment era debated the authenticity of the "satanic verses" mentioned in early Islamic texts, reflecting the era's skepticism towards religious doctrine and the quest for historical accuracy. The controversy surrounding these verses highlighted broader debates about the reliability of religious texts and the intersection of faith and reason in the pursuit of truth.

The 'Philosophical Duel' of Diderot and Rousseau: Denis Diderot and Jean-Jacques Rousseau engaged in a philosophical duel through their writings, exchanging critiques and disagreements about topics such as civilization, morality, and the nature of humanity. This intellectual rivalry exemplified the passionate and competitive nature of Enlightenment discourse, as well as the diversity of perspectives within the philosophical community.

The Alchemists of the Enlightenment

Despite the rise of empirical science during the Enlightenment, some intellectuals continued to practice alchemy, seeking to transmute base metals into gold and discover the philosopher's stone. This persistence in alchemical pursuits, often dismissed as pseudoscience, reflects the era's fascination with hidden knowledge and the boundaries between science and mysticism.

The Literary Hoaxes of the Enlightenment: Enlightenment-era authors, such as Horace Walpole and Thomas Chatterton, perpetrated literary hoaxes that fooled their contemporaries and challenged notions of authenticity and authorship. These hoaxes, which included forged manuscripts and fictional personas, blurred the lines between reality and fiction, reflecting the era's preoccupation with literary invention.

The Rise of Coffeehouse Culture: Coffeehouses became hubs of intellectual activity during the Enlightenment, fostering lively debates and discussions among scholars, writers, and philosophers. This vibrant coffeehouse culture facilitated the exchange of ideas and information, democratizing access to knowledge and contributing to the spread of Enlightenment ideals.

The Philosopher's Garden: During the Enlightenment period, intellectuals and philosophers sought to create spaces that reflected their philosophical ideals. These "philosopher's gardens" were meticulously designed to incorporate elements of symbolism and allegory, representing philosophical concepts such as reason, harmony, and natural order. For example, geometrically arranged flowerbeds symbolize the rationality and orderliness of the universe, while meandering paths could evoke the unpredictability of human experience. These gardens served as places of leisure but also as outdoor classrooms where scholars engage in discussions about the nature of existence, morality, and the human condition.

The Vegetable Lamb of Tartary: The legend exemplifies the blend of scientific inquiry and fantastical imagination prevalent during the Enlightenment. Originating from medieval folklore, the belief in a plant that grew sheep as its fruit captured the era's fascination with natural wonders and exploration. While it may seem absurd to modern sensibilities, this myth reflects the era's efforts to reconcile scientific curiosity with mythical traditions.

The Industrial Revolution

Child Labor in Chimney Sweeping: During the early Industrial Revolution, child labor was rampant, with children as young as four or five years old employed as chimney sweeps. These children, known as "climbing boys," were forced to climb inside narrow chimneys to clean soot and ash, often enduring hazardous conditions and suffering from respiratory problems.

The "Mule Spinner Riot": In 1831, textile workers in Lancashire, England, known as "mule spinners," rioted against the introduction of new machinery that threatened their livelihoods. The protests escalated into violent clashes with authorities, resulting in arrests and widespread disruption to factory operations.

The Luddite Movement: The Luddites were a group of English textile workers and skilled artisans who protested the mechanization of textile production during the early 19th century. Named after Ned Ludd, a mythical figure said to have destroyed weaving machinery, the Luddites sabotaged factories and machinery in a futile attempt to preserve traditional craftsmanship.

The Pneumatic Railway: In the 1860s, the first experimental pneumatic railway was built in London, utilizing compressed air to propel trains through underground tunnels. Despite initial enthusiasm, the project faced technical challenges and financial difficulties, leading to its eventual abandonment after a few years of operation.

The Factory Acts: In response to the harsh working conditions endured by laborers during the Industrial Revolution, the British government introduced a series of Factory Acts between 1802 and 1833 to regulate child labor, working hours, and workplace safety.

These laws marked early attempts to address social and humanitarian concerns arising from industrialization.

The Spinning Jenny Patent Dispute: James Hargreaves, inventor of the spinning jenny, faced legal challenges from rival manufacturers who sought to invalidate his patent and produce similar machines. The ensuing legal battles highlighted the complexities of intellectual property rights and the fierce competition among inventors during the Industrial Revolution.

Phossy Jaw Epidemic: Phossy jaw, a debilitating condition characterized by necrosis of the jawbone, afflicted thousands of match factory workers exposed to phosphorus fumes during the 19th century. Despite evidence of the health risks associated with phosphorus-based matches, manufacturers resisted regulations until public outcry led to the eventual ban of phosphorus in match production.

The Great Stink of London: In 1858, London was engulfed by a foul odor emanating from the polluted River Thames, exacerbated by rapid industrialization and untreated sewage disposal. The stench became so unbearable that it prompted the British government to undertake ambitious engineering projects, including the construction of the London sewer system, to mitigate the problem.

The Spinning Mule's Impact on Poetry: Samuel Crompton's invention of the spinning mule, which combined features of the spinning jenny and the water frame, revolutionized textile production and inspired literary works such as William Blake's poem "Jerusalem." The poem's reference to "dark satanic mills" reflects Blake's critique of the dehumanizing effects of industrialization.

The Rocket's Influence on Railways: George Stephenson's steam locomotive, the Rocket, played a crucial role in the development of railways and transportation networks during the Industrial Revolution. Its innovative design, featuring a Mult tubular boiler and steam blast pipe, setting new standards for locomotive performance and efficiency.

The Crystal Palace Dinosaurs

The Crystal Palace Dinosaurs, a series of sculpted dinosaur models commissioned for the Great Exhibition of 1851 in London, represented the first attempt to depict prehistoric creatures in a public exhibition. Created by artist Benjamin Waterhouse Hawkins, these concrete and iron sculptures sparked public fascination with paleontology and inspired the modern field of dinosaur studies. Today, these sculptures stand as a testament to both the artistic creativity of the Victorian era and the enduring allure of dinosaurs as symbols of Earth's ancient past.

The Puddling Process: The puddling process, developed by Henry Cort in the late 18th century, revolutionized iron production by enabling the extraction of impurities from pig iron to produce malleable wrought iron. This innovation played a pivotal role in the expansion of the iron and steel industry during the Industrial Revolution, facilitating the construction of bridges, railways, and machinery.

The Flying Shuttle Riot: In 1769, textile workers in Lancashire, England, protested against the introduction of John Kay's flying shuttle, which increased the speed of weaving and threatened traditional handloom weavers' livelihoods. The riots resulted in clashes with authorities and the destruction of newly installed machinery.

The Cotton Famine: During the American Civil War (1861-1865), the Union's blockade of Confederate ports disrupted cotton exports to Britain, leading to a shortage of raw materials for the textile industry. This "cotton famine" caused widespread unemployment and economic hardship in northern England, highlighting the region's dependence on imported cotton.

The Founding of Model Industrial Towns: Industrialists such as Robert Owen and Titus Salt established model industrial towns, such as New Lanark in Scotland and Saltaire in England, to provide better living and working conditions for factory workers. These planned communities featured improved housing, sanitation, and social amenities, reflecting early efforts to address the social consequences of industrialization.

The Rise of Industrial Espionage: As competition intensified among industrialists during the Industrial Revolution, espionage and sabotage became common tactics for gaining a competitive edge. Industrial spies, often employed by rival firms, infiltrated factories to steal trade secrets or disrupt production processes, leading to heightened security measures and legal battles.

The Iron Bridge

The construction of the Iron Bridge over the River Severn in Shropshire, England, in 1779 marked a significant engineering achievement and symbolized the transition from traditional to industrial methods of bridge building. Designed by architect Thomas Farnolls Pritchard and built by ironmaster Abraham Darby III, the bridge showcased the potential of iron as a structural material and inspired future infrastructure projects worldwide. Today, the Iron Bridge stands as a UNESCO World Heritage Site, commemorating its historical significance and enduring legacy in the development of modern engineering practices.

The Penny Black Stamp: The Penny Black, issued in 1840, was the world's first adhesive postage stamp, introduced in Britain to facilitate the efficient processing of mail during the Industrial Revolution. Designed by postal reformer Rowland Hill, the stamp featured a profile of Queen Victoria and revolutionized postal systems by standardizing postage rates and prepayment.

The Factory Acts and Women's Rights: The Factory Acts of the 19th century, while primarily focused on improving working conditions and curtailing exploitation in industrial settings, had significant implications for women's rights. By limiting the hours and conditions under which women and children could work in factories, these laws inadvertently sparked discussions about gender equality, economic empowerment, and social justice. As women found themselves excluded from certain industries due to legislative restrictions, it fueled their participation in the burgeoning women's rights movement, prompting calls for equal opportunities, access to education, and labor reform. Consequently, the Factory Acts laid the groundwork for modern labor regulations.

The Impact of the Industrial Revolution on Global Trade: The Industrial Revolution had a profound impact on global trade dynamics, reshaping the landscape of commerce and ushering in a new era of interconnectedness between nations. As industrialization accelerated in Western Europe and North America, there was a surge in demand for raw materials such as cotton, coal, and iron ore, leading to increased trade with resource-rich regions around the world. This heightened demand for raw materials spurred colonial expansion and exploitation, as European powers sought to secure access to valuable resources in Africa, Asia, and the Americas. Consequently, the Industrial Revolution not only transformed the economic fortunes of industrialized nations but also fueled the rise of imperialism and colonialism, shaping the course of global trade for centuries to come.

World War I

Trench mascots: Life in the trenches was bleak and often devoid of comforts, so soldiers on both sides found solace in the companionship of animals. The British army embraced the idea of trench mascots, which included dogs, cats, and even a bear named Winnie. These animals provided much-needed emotional support and camaraderie amidst the horrors of war.

Spoof newspapers: Propaganda played a significant role in shaping public opinion during World War I, and both sides engaged in efforts to undermine enemy morale. The British employed a creative tactic by distributing fake newspapers filled with humorous and satirical articles, designed to ridicule the enemy and boost morale among their own troops.

Camouflage Corps: As trench warfare became increasingly entrenched, camouflage became a crucial aspect of military strategy. The United States Army established a specialized unit known as the Camouflage Corps, tasked with creating elaborate and surreal camouflage designs to conceal military installations from enemy observation. These innovative camouflage techniques helped to deceive and confuse enemy forces, contributing to the success of Allied operations.

Christmas Truce of 1914: Perhaps one of the most remarkable moments of humanity amidst the brutality of World War I was the spontaneous Christmas Truce of 1914. Soldiers from opposing trenches along the Western Front laid down their weapons, exchanged gifts, and even played soccer matches in no man's land. This temporary ceasefire demonstrated the shared humanity of soldiers on both sides and served as a poignant reminder of the futility of war.

Pigeon-guided missiles

The concept of using pigeons as missile guides during World War I reflected the desperate search for innovative military strategies, but it faced numerous challenges, including the difficulty of training pigeons for such tasks and the unreliable nature of their guidance. Despite initial experimentation, practical limitations and the advent of more advanced technologies led to the abandonment of this unconventional warfare method. Nonetheless, the brief exploration of pigeon-guided missiles serves as a curious footnote in the history of military innovation during the Great War.

Pigeon soldiers: Communication was essential for coordinating military operations during World War I, especially in the chaos of trench warfare. The French army utilized carrier pigeons equipped with miniature cameras or message capsules to transmit vital information behind enemy lines. These "pigeon soldiers" played a crucial role in maintaining communication networks and providing intelligence to military commanders.

Q-ships: The British Royal Navy employed a clever tactic to counter German U-boats during World War I by using disguised merchant vessels known as Q-ships. These ships were armed with concealed guns and posed as vulnerable targets to lure unsuspecting U-boats into ambushes. The element of surprise often led to successful engagements, as U-boats were caught off guard by the hidden firepower of the Q-ships.

Camouflage makeup: In the trenches, soldiers faced constant threats from snipers and enemy observation posts, leading to the development of various camouflage techniques. One unconventional method was the use of camouflage makeup, with soldiers applying dark grease or paint to their faces to blend into the mud and shadows of the trenches. This simple yet effective tactic helped to conceal soldiers from enemy sight and reduce the risk of detection.

Attack dogs: German forces experimented with the use of attack dogs fitted with explosives strapped to their backs as a means of breaching enemy defenses. These dogs were trained to run towards enemy positions and detonate upon reaching their targets, causing chaos and confusion among opposing troops. However, the effectiveness of this tactic was limited by the dogs' reluctance to charge into gunfire and the risk of premature detonation.

Faked death kits: In the dangerous world of espionage and covert operations, deception was often a key strategy for infiltrating enemy lines. British intelligence agents developed "faked death kits," providing soldiers with elaborate disguises and props to simulate their deaths and escape from behind enemy lines. These kits were used in daring operations to gather intelligence and conduct sabotage missions deep within enemy territory.

Trench musicians: Despite the grim conditions of trench warfare, soldiers found ways to maintain their spirits through music and camaraderie. The British Army organized units of "trench musicians," equipped with instruments such as harmonicas, bugles, and drums, to provide entertainment and boost morale in the trenches. Music served as a form of emotional release and solidarity among soldiers facing the hardships of war.

War dogs: Dogs have a long history of serving alongside humans in warfare, and World War I was no exception. The French army trained war dogs for various roles, including carrying messages, locating wounded soldiers, and detecting enemy gas attacks on the battlefield. These loyal and brave animals played a vital role in supporting troops and saving lives during the conflict.

Fake trees: As part of their efforts to conceal military installations from enemy observation, soldiers on both sides employed creative camouflage techniques. The French army constructed "fake trees" made from steel or wire frames covered with painted canvas to disguise observation posts and snipers in no man's land. These camouflaged structures blended seamlessly into the landscape, making them difficult for enemy observers to detect.

Spy kits: Espionage and sabotage played a significant role in World War I, with both sides employing spies and covert operatives to gather intelligence and disrupt enemy activities. British intelligence agents equipped soldiers with "spy kits," containing disguises, forged documents, and other espionage tools to facilitate clandestine operations behind enemy lines. These kits were used in daring missions to gather intelligence and sabotage enemy infrastructure.

Dummy airfields: Deception was a critical element of military strategy during World War I, and both sides employed elaborate ruses to confuse and mislead their enemies. British and German forces constructed "dummy airfields" with fake aircraft, hangars, and runways to deceive enemy reconnaissance planes. These decoy installations diverted enemy bombers away from real targets, reducing the effectiveness of aerial attacks.

Anti-submarine kites

The threat of enemy submarines posed a significant challenge for naval forces during World War I, leading to the development of innovative countermeasures. The British Navy experimented with "anti-submarine kites," large kites equipped with explosives or depth charges, which were towed behind ships to target and destroy enemy submarines lurking beneath the surface. These unconventional weapons helped to protect allied vessels from submarine attacks and disrupt enemy naval operations.

Rat bombs: During World War I, the trenches were not only battlegrounds for soldiers but also breeding grounds for disease-carrying vermin, particularly rats, which thrived in the squalid and unsanitary environment. To capitalize on this nuisance, British intelligence agents conceived the idea of "rat bombs," a clandestine weapon disguised as dead rats. These explosive devices were designed to exploit the pervasive presence of rats in enemy trenches, as soldiers would often dismiss dead rodents without suspicion. The intention was to sow fear and confusion among enemy troops by deploying these covert explosives in strategic locations, adding a psychological dimension to the warfare tactics of the time. While the historical record is sparse on the actual deployment and effectiveness of rat bombs, their existence serves as a testament to the ingenuity and innovation born out of the exigencies of war.

Trench art: Amidst the chaos and destruction of war, soldiers sought solace and distraction through creative expression. "Trench art" refers to artwork created by soldiers using materials readily available in the trenches, such as shell casings, bullets, and scraps of metal. These works of art served as a form of therapy, allowing soldiers to process their experiences and maintain a sense of humanity amidst the brutality of war.

Cigarette gas masks: The threat of poison gas attacks was a constant fear for soldiers in the trenches, prompting them to devise makeshift methods of protection. One such innovation was the "cigarette gas mask," constructed from cloth or handkerchiefs soaked in chemicals or urine to act as crude filters against toxic gasses. While not as effective as standard-issue gas masks, these improvised devices provided some degree of protection in emergencies. These improvised devices served as a stark reminder of the harsh realities of trench warfare and the constant need for innovative solutions to mitigate the dangers faced on the battlefield.

The Roaring Twenties

Monkey Trials: The Scopes Monkey Trial of 1925 was a landmark case in which high school teacher John Scopes was prosecuted for teaching evolution in violation of Tennessee's Butler Act. The trial became a national sensation, with renowned lawyers Clarence Darrow and William Jennings Bryan facing off in a courtroom battle over the teaching of evolution in public schools.

The Smell of Wealth: Despite Prohibition banning the sale and consumption of alcohol, the wealthy elite in New York found creative ways to indulge in their favorite libations. Perfumes and colognes containing high concentrations of alcohol became a fashionable way for the upper class to flaunt their wealth and flout the law.

Pet Alligators: In the 1920s, alligators became an unexpected trend in the United States, with many people bringing them home as exotic pets after visiting Florida. However, the novelty quickly wore off as owners realized that alligators are not suitable domestic animals, leading to many of them being abandoned or released into the wild.

Dance Marathons: Dance marathons, also known as endurance contests or walkathons, became popular entertainment events during the Great Depression. Couples would dance for hours, days, or even weeks at a time, competing for cash prizes and enduring physical exhaustion and sleep deprivation in the hopes of winning fame and fortune.

Hollywoodland: The iconic Hollywood sign originally read "Hollywoodland" and was erected in 1923 as an advertisement for a real estate development in the Hollywood Hills. Over time, the sign became synonymous with the glamor and allure of the film industry, and the "land" portion was eventually removed, leaving behind the iconic landmark we know today.

Auto Polo

Auto polo, a spectacle of the 1920s, epitomized the era's fascination with speed and daring exploits, melding the genteel sport of polo with the adrenaline rush of automobile races. The game featured players piloting specially modified cars, typically stripped down for agility and speed, across a makeshift arena resembling a polo field. Maneuvering their vehicles with skill and audacity, competitors wielded long mallets to strike a ball, striving for goals amidst the chaos of roaring engines and swerving vehicles. Despite its popularity as a spectator sport, auto polo was rife with danger, as collisions, flips, and spills were common occurrences, often resulting in injuries to both players and bystanders. Nonetheless, its brief heyday captured the spirit of an era defined by innovation, risk-taking, and a thirst for excitement on the cusp of modernity.

Cocaine in Coca-Cola: In the early 20th century, Coca-Cola contained small amounts of cocaine derived from coca leaves. While the cocaine content was negligible and legal at the time, changing regulations and social attitudes towards drugs led the company to remove it from the recipe in 1929.

Radioactive Health Products: Radioactive health products, such as radium-infused water and cosmetics, gained popularity in the 1920s, with manufacturers touting their supposed rejuvenating and curative properties. However, the dangers of radiation exposure were not fully understood at the time, leading to widespread use of these products with harmful consequences for consumers.

Flaming Youth: "Flaming youth" was a term coined in the 1920s to describe the rebellious and carefree attitude of young people, particularly women, who embraced newfound freedoms and challenged traditional societal norms. The term was popularized by the 1923 film "Flaming Youth," starring Colleen Moore, which depicted the exploits of a young, independent woman navigating the social and cultural changes of the era.

The Harlem Renaissance: The Harlem Renaissance was a flourishing of African American art, music, literature, and culture that took place in the 1920s. Centered in the Harlem neighborhood of New York City, the movement produced iconic works by artists such as Langston Hughes, Zora Neale Hurston, and Duke Ellington, celebrating African American heritage and identity in the face of systemic racism and discrimination. The Harlem Renaissance not only left an indelible mark on American culture but also served as a catalyst for the Civil Rights Movement, inspiring generations to fight against racial injustice and oppression. Its legacy continues to resonate today, reminding us of the power of artistic expression as tool for social change and the importance of celebrating diverse voices and experiences.

The Great Molasses Flood

The Great Molasses Flood of 1919 was a tragic industrial accident in Boston, Massachusetts, where a massive storage tank burst, releasing millions of gallons of molasses into the streets. The fast-moving wave of molasses, traveling at speeds of up to 35 miles per hour, destroyed buildings, overturned vehicles, and claimed the lives of 21 people, leaving a sticky and devastating aftermath. The once-bustling streets of Boston were transformed into a scene reminiscent of a disaster movie, with buildings collapsed like houses of cards and debris strewn everywhere, all coated in a thick, viscous layer of molasses. The cleanup efforts were daunting, as workers faced the arduous task of removing sticky residue from every surface, including cobblestone streets and the interiors of homes and businesses.

Rum Row: During Prohibition, "Rum Row" became a notorious hotspot for clandestine activities, transforming the tranquil waters off the U.S. coast into a bustling marketplace for bootlegged liquor. The term "rum row" evoked the clandestine nature of the operation, with ships anchored just beyond U.S. territorial waters, beyond the reach of law enforcement. These vessels, often sleek and fast, were dubbed "rum runners," their decks laden with crates of contraband liquor sourced from countries where alcohol remained legal. The cat-and-mouse game between rum runners and Coast Guard patrols intensified, with rum runners employing various tactics to evade detection, including nighttime operations and decoy vessels. The lucrative trade on Rum Row not only fueled the speakeasy culture onshore but also lined the pockets of smugglers and organized crime syndicates, illustrating the resilience of the human spirit in the face of prohibitionist policies.

The Lost Generation: Coined by writer Gertrude Stein, the term "Lost Generation" referred to disillusioned American writers and artists who came of age during World War I and felt disconnected from traditional values and societal norms. Writers such as Ernest Hemingway, F. Scott Fitzgerald, and Gertrude Stein herself were prominent figures of the Lost Generation, exploring themes of alienation, disillusionment, and existential despair in their works.

Jazz Age: The 1920s were often referred to as the Jazz Age, a period characterized by the vibrant music, dance, and culture that emerged in cities like New Orleans, Chicago, and New York. Jazz music, with its improvisational style and syncopated rhythms, became synonymous with the spirit of the era, influencing everything from fashion and nightlife to social attitudes and racial relations.

Spiritualism: Spiritualism experienced a resurgence in the 1920s, with many people turning to mediums, seances, and Ouija boards in search of comfort and connection with the spirit world. The trauma of World War I and the Spanish Flu pandemic, combined with advancements in technology and communication, fueled interest in spiritualism as people sought answers to life's existential questions and solace in the face of uncertainty.

Flagpole Sitting Fad

Flagpole sitting was a bizarre craze that swept across America in the 1920s, with individuals attempting to set endurance records by perching atop tall flagpoles for days or even weeks at a time.

The fad was fueled by a desire for fame and notoriety, with participants enduring physical discomfort and exposure to the elements in pursuit of their goals. Despite its popularity, flagpole sitting was eventually deemed too dangerous and fell out of favor, leaving behind a curious footnote in the history of American fads and stunts.

The Sheik Craze: The success of the 1921 film "The Sheik," starring Rudolph Valentino as a dashing Arab sheik, sparked a cultural phenomenon known as the "sheik craze." Audiences were captivated by the romanticized portrayal of the exotic and mysterious Middle East, leading to a surge in interest in all things Arabian, from fashion and home decor to literature and entertainment.

The Florida Land Boom: The Florida land boom of the 1920s was a speculative frenzy fueled by dreams of quick wealth and prosperity. Investors from across the country flocked to Florida to buy up land, leading to skyrocketing prices and rampant speculation. However, the bubble burst in 1926, triggering a devastating collapse in land values and leaving many investors bankrupt.

The Radium Girls

Tragedy unfolded in the early 20th century when young women were employed to paint watch dials with luminous radium paint, a job considered prestigious due to the glow-in-the-dark effect of the paint. Unfortunately, they were not informed about the dangers of radium exposure, and many ingested or inhaled the radioactive substance while shaping the fine paintbrushes with their lips, a technique known as "lip-pointing." As a result, they suffered from devastating health effects, including radiation poisoning, bone fractures, and necrosis of the jaw, leading to the term "radium jaw." Despite their deteriorating health, the Radium Girls fought for justice against the companies that had exposed them to the toxic substance. Their legal battles and advocacy efforts ultimately led to landmark changes in occupational safety standards, including regulations on the handling of hazardous materials and the rights of workers to a safe workplace.

The Cold War Era

Project Acoustic Kitty: During the Cold War, the CIA attempted to turn cats into covert listening devices in a project known as "Acoustic Kitty." The project involved surgically implanting microphones and transmitters into cats, but it was ultimately deemed a failure due to the difficulty of training the felines and their unpredictable behavior.

The Soviet "Dead Hand" System: The Soviet Union developed a doomsday device known as the "Dead Hand" or "Perimeter" system, designed to automatically launch nuclear missiles in the event of a decapitating strike on the Soviet leadership. This system operated on the principle of assured retaliation, ensuring mutual destruction even if Soviet leaders were incapacitated.

Operation Gladio: NATO's secret "stay-behind" armies, collectively known as Operation Gladio, was established during the Cold War to conduct guerrilla warfare behind enemy lines in the event of a Soviet invasion of Western Europe. However, these clandestine networks were also involved in various covert operations, including acts of terrorism and destabilization, leading to controversy and conspiracy theories.

The "Red Telephone" Misconception: Contrary to popular belief, the hotline established between the United States and the Soviet Union during the Cold War was not a direct telephone line but rather a teletype link. This system, officially known as the "Washington-Moscow Direct Communications Link," was intended to facilitate communication and reduce the risk of misinterpretation during times of crisis. Despite its nickname, the "Red Telephone" was a symbolic representation of the urgent communication channel rather than a literal phone line, underscoring the complexities of diplomatic relations between the two superpowers. This misconception highlights the enduring impact of Cold War imagery on public perception and the need for accurate historical context when examining geopolitical history.

The Coca-Cola Bottle as a Symbol of Capitalism

The iconic Coca-Cola bottle, with its distinctive contour and red branding, became more than just a vessel for a fizzy beverage; it symbolized the American way of life and capitalist ideals. As tensions between the United States and the Soviet Union escalated during the Cold War, the Coca-Cola bottle became a potent emblem of Western consumerism and cultural influence, contrasting starkly with the austere imagery promoted by communist regimes. In response to this perceived threat, Soviet authorities launched propaganda campaigns denouncing Coca-Cola as a symbol of capitalist decadence and exploitation, attempting to discourage its consumption among citizens of the Eastern Bloc. Despite these efforts, the allure of Coca-Cola proved irresistible to many people behind the Iron Curtain, leading to a thriving black market for the coveted beverage. In underground economies, individuals would go to great lengths to acquire Coca-Cola, smuggling it across borders or trading scarce resources for a taste of the forbidden soda.

The Sino-Soviet Split: Despite their ideological alignment as communist powers, the Soviet Union and China experienced a bitter rift known as the Sino-Soviet Split during the Cold War. Tensions between the two countries escalated over ideological differences, border disputes, and leadership rivalries, leading to a breakdown in relations and even armed clashes along their shared border.

Operation Paul Bunyan: In response to the killing of two U.S. soldiers by North Korean forces in the Korean Demilitarized Zone (DMZ) in 1976, the United States launched Operation Paul Bunyan, a massive show of force that involved the deployment of troops, helicopters, and armored vehicles to chop down a tree in the DMZ. This seemingly disproportionate response aimed to assert U.S. military dominance and deter further aggression.

The Bear Incident at Vandenberg Air Force Base: In 1962, a bear managed to breach the security perimeter of Vandenberg Air Force Base in California, leading to a series of comical mishaps as military personnel attempted to capture the intruding animal. Despite the Cold War tensions of the time, the bear incident provided a moment of levity and served as a reminder of the unpredictability of nature amidst the specter of nuclear conflict.

The CIA's Espionage Cat: In the 1960s, the CIA attempted to train cats as espionage agents by implanting listening devices into their bodies and deploying them to eavesdrop on conversations in sensitive locations. However, the project, codenamed "Operation Acoustic Kitty," was ultimately abandoned due to the challenges of training the cats and the unpredictability of their behavior.

Nuclear-Powered Satellite Proposals: During the Cold War, both the United States and the Soviet Union explored the concept of nuclear-powered satellites as a means of extending the duration and capabilities of space missions. However, concerns over the safety and environmental impact of nuclear reactors in orbit led to the abandonment of these proposals.

The "Space Pen" Myth: Contrary to popular belief, NASA did not spend millions of dollars developing a special pen that could write in zero gravity, while the Soviets used pencils. Both NASA and the Soviet space program initially used pencils, but concerns over graphite particles and flammability led to the development of a pressurized ink pen by a private company, which NASA later adopted.

The Bizarre Plan to Nuke the Moon: During the Cold War, the United States considered a plan known as "Project A119," which aimed to detonate a nuclear bomb on the Moon as a show of force and technological superiority against the Soviet Union. While the project was ultimately shelved due to concerns over the potential environmental and political consequences, it remains a testament to the extreme measures considered during the Cold War.

The Soviet Woodpecker Signal: In the 1970s and 1980s, amateur radio operators worldwide began picking up a mysterious tapping noise on certain frequencies, which came to be known as the "Woodpecker Signal" due to its distinctive pattern. It was later revealed to be a Soviet over-the-horizon radar system, part of the Duga radar network, intended to detect incoming missiles and aircraft.

The Mysterious "Numbers Stations": Throughout the Cold War and beyond, shortwave radio stations known as "numbers stations" broadcast coded messages, typically consisting of strings of numbers or letters, believed to be intended for espionage purposes. Despite efforts by intelligence agencies to monitor and decipher these transmissions, the true purpose and origin of numbers stations remain shrouded in secrecy.

The Lysenko Affair

Trofim Lysenko's rise to prominence within the Soviet Union's scientific community marked a dark chapter in the nation's history, characterized by the suppression of legitimate scientific inquiry in favor of politically expedient ideology. Exploiting his close ties to the Communist Party leadership, Lysenko ruthlessly purged dissenting voices from the scientific establishment, effectively silencing critics and monopolizing agricultural research. Under his influence, Soviet agriculture was subjected to pseudoscientific experiments and impractical methods, such as wide-spacing planting and vernalization, which disregarded the genetic diversity and ecological requirements of crops. The consequences of Lysenko's misguided policies were catastrophic, as they contributed to widespread crop failures, reduced agricultural productivity, and exacerbated food shortages, particularly during periods of famine. Ultimately, Lysenko's pseudo-scientific legacy serves as a cautionary tale about the dangers of subordinating scientific truth to ideological dogma and the profound consequences of politicizing scientific research.

The Secret Soviet Moon Missions: In the 1960s, the Soviet Union embarked on a series of secret moon missions known as the "Zond program," which aimed to test spacecraft systems and gather lunar reconnaissance data. These missions remained classified for decades, highlighting the clandestine nature of space exploration during the Cold War.

The Great Emu War: In 1932, Australia experienced a bizarre conflict known as the "Great Emu War," where the Australian military deployed soldiers armed with machine guns to combat a large population of emus that were causing crop damage. Despite their efforts, the emus proved elusive, and the military's campaign was ultimately ineffective, resulting in widespread ridicule.

The Stasi's "Smell Samples": The East German secret police, known as the Stasi, developed a bizarre surveillance technique involving the collection of scent samples from targeted individuals. These "smell samples" were stored in jars and used by trained dogs to track and identify suspects, demonstrating the lengths to which authoritarian regimes would go to maintain control over their citizens.

The "Pig War" Between the U.S. and USSR: In 1959, a bizarre incident known as the "Pig War" occurred between the United States and the Soviet Union when an American military officer stationed in West Berlin received a shipment of pigs from the U.S. as part of a breeding program. The Soviet authorities detained the animals for several months, leading to a diplomatic standoff between the two superpowers. This peculiar episode underscored the absurdities of Cold War rivalries and the lengths to which both sides would go to assert dominance.

The CIA's Use of Magic Tricks: During the Cold War, the CIA explored the use of stage magic and sleight of hand techniques for covert operations and psychological warfare. Magicians were recruited to teach agents techniques such as misdirection, sleight of hand, and covert communication, with the aim of enhancing espionage capabilities and deceiving adversaries.

Space Exploration

Lost Cosmonaut Conspiracy: During the early days of space exploration, rumors circulated about Soviet cosmonauts who supposedly died in secret missions that were covered up by the government. These alleged "lost cosmonauts" became the subject of conspiracy theories, though evidence supporting their existence remains scant.

Space Pen Myth: Contrary to popular belief, NASA did not spend millions of dollars developing a pen that could write in space; rather, Paul Fisher, an inventor, independently developed the Fisher Space Pen using his own funds. The pen uses a pressurized ink cartridge to write in zero-gravity environments, and both NASA and the Soviet space program adopted it for their missions.

Golden Record on Voyager: Voyager 1 and Voyager 2 spacecraft each carry a golden record containing sounds and images representing Earth, intended as a message to any extraterrestrial civilizations that might encounter them. This interstellar time capsule includes greetings in 55 languages, music from different cultures, and natural sounds of Earth, curated by a committee chaired by Carl Sagan.

Space Dust Collection by Stardust: NASA's Stardust spacecraft collected samples of interstellar dust during its mission, capturing particles from beyond our solar system. These microscopic grains, traveling at speeds of over 20,000 kilometers per hour, provided valuable insights into the composition and origins of interstellar matter. The painstaking analysis of these interstellar particles not only expanded our understanding of the universe but also demonstrated the ingenuity and technical prowess of NASA's scientific endeavors, pushing the boundaries of what was thought possible in space exploration.

Space Bat on Space Shuttle

The discovery of a bat clinging to the external fuel tank of the Space Shuttle Discovery just before the STS-119 mission's launch in 2009 highlighted the unforeseen encounters with wildlife that astronauts and engineers face in space exploration. The presence of the bat, likely seeking refuge in the shuttle's structures during pre-launch preparations, underscored the challenges of maintaining secure and controlled environments in the complex infrastructure of space vehicles. This unexpected incident prompted NASA to enhance wildlife mitigation measures and reinforce habitat control protocols to minimize the risk of similar occurrences in future missions. Additionally, the incident sparked discussions about the potential impacts of wildlife on spacecraft operations and the importance of comprehensive risk management strategies in space exploration endeavors

Space Sickness Remedies: Astronauts often experience space sickness, a phenomenon like motion sickness caused by changes in vestibular function in microgravity. To alleviate symptoms, NASA developed a range of remedies, including medications, special diets, and relaxation techniques, to ensure crew members' well-being during space missions.

Frozen Frog on Space Shuttle: In 1995, a frog inadvertently hitched a ride on Space Shuttle Endeavour during its STS-54 mission. The frog likely sought refuge in the spacecraft's structures, but unfortunately, it did not survive the extreme temperatures of space and was found frozen upon discovery.

Space Gardens on Mir: Russian cosmonauts on the Mir space station cultivated space gardens to study the effects of microgravity on plant growth and food production. These hydroponic gardens provided fresh vegetables and herbs for the crew's consumption, contributing to research on sustainable food sources for long-duration space missions.

Space Whiskey Aging Experiment: In 2011, Ardbeg Distillery partnered with Nano Racks to send vials of whiskey samples to the International Space Station for a unique aging experiment. The microgravity environment accelerated chemical reactions, leading to novel flavors and aromas in the whiskey, offering insights into new methods of spirit production.

Cosmic Ray Observations on Apollo Missions: During the Apollo missions to the Moon, astronauts observed strange flashes of light when they closed their eyes in the darkness of space. These phenomena were later identified as cosmic ray particles passing through their retinas, providing valuable data for understanding space radiation hazards.

Space Artifacts Theft: Over the years, numerous space artifacts, including moon rocks and space suits, have been stolen from museums and government facilities. Some of these items have been recovered, but others remain missing, highlighting the challenges of preserving and safeguarding historic objects from space exploration.

Space Art on Moon Missions

Astronauts on the Apollo missions left behind artistic mementos on the Moon, including drawings, sculptures, and even a small figurine known as the "Fallen Astronaut." These symbolic gestures served as expressions of human creativity and exploration, commemorating their historic journeys to the lunar surface.

Space Bacteria Discovery: Scientists discovered bacteria thriving on the exterior surfaces of the International Space Station, known as extremophiles due to their ability to survive harsh conditions. These microorganisms, including the species of Deinococcus and Acinetobacter, have implications for planetary protection protocols and the search for extraterrestrial life. Furthermore, studying these extremophiles could provide valuable insights into how life might survive and evolve in extreme environments beyond Earth, informing future astrobiological research endeavors and our understanding of the potential habitability of other celestial bodies.

Space Music Composition: Composer Gerald Jay Markoe created "Symphony of the Planets," a series of musical compositions based on electromagnetic waves captured by NASA spacecraft exploring the solar system. These recordings, converted into audible frequencies, offer listeners an immersive journey through the celestial soundscape of our cosmic neighborhood.

Space Artifacts Replicas: To preserve historic space artifacts while allowing public access, museums and institutions often display replicas of lunar rocks, space capsules, and other significant objects. These meticulously crafted replicas provide visitors with tangible experiences of space exploration history while protecting priceless originals.

Space Hibernation Research: Scientists are exploring the possibility of inducing hibernation-like states in astronauts during long-duration space missions to conserve resources and mitigate physiological effects of space travel. This research draws inspiration from hibernating animals and aims to develop medical techniques for inducing torpor or suspended animation in humans. By manipulating metabolic processes and lowering body temperature, scientists hope to create a state of suspended animation that could significantly reduce the physical and psychological toll of space travel on astronauts.

Space Oddity Tribute: Astronaut Chris Hadfield recorded a cover of David Bowie's song "Space Oddity" aboard the International Space Station in 2013. The music video, featuring Hadfield singing and playing guitar in microgravity, became a viral sensation and a poignant tribute to Bowie's legacy of space-themed music.

Space Artifacts Repatriation: Several countries, including the United States and Russia, have repatriated lunar samples and other space artifacts gifted to foreign dignitaries during the Apollo era. These artifacts, originally presented as goodwill gestures, are now housed in national museums and institutions, symbolizing international cooperation in space exploration. The repatriation of lunar samples and space artifacts reflects a growing recognition of their historical and scientific significance, as well as a desire to preserve and study them within their respective countries. This process not only safeguards these valuable relics for future generations but also fosters a sense of national pride and ownership in humanity's collective journey beyond Earth's bounds, highlighting the enduring legacy of space exploration as a shared endeavor of all nations.

Space Tardigrades: Tardigrades, microscopic creatures known for their resilience, were sent into space aboard the European Space Agency's FOTON-M3 mission in 2007. These extremophiles survived exposure to the vacuum of space and cosmic radiation, demonstrating their remarkable adaptability to extreme environments. The inclusion of tardigrades in the FOTON-M3 mission not only showcased their extraordinary survival capabilities but also raised ethical concerns about the unintentional spread of life beyond Earth. Despite their resilience, the ethical implications of potentially contaminating other celestial bodies with terrestrial lifeforms prompted debates within the scientific community regarding the responsible exploration of space and the preservation of extraterrestrial environments.

Space Spider Web Formation: On the International Space Station, spiders introduced for scientific experiments were observed spinning asymmetric webs due to the absence of gravity. These unusual web structures provided insights into the influence of gravity on arachnid behavior and silk production.

Astonishing Discoveries in Archaeology

The Great Zimbabwe Ruins: Located in present-day Zimbabwe, the Great Zimbabwe ruins are the remains of an ancient city built by the Shona people between the 11th and 15th centuries CE. The site's impressive stone structures, including the Great Enclosure, suggest it was a center of trade, religion, and political power in medieval Africa.

The Lost City of Petra: Hidden within the rugged desert canyons of Jordan, the Lost City of Petra is a breathtaking archaeological site renowned for its intricate rock-cut architecture and water management systems. Rediscovered by Western explorers in the early 19th century, Petra was once a thriving trading hub and capital of the Nabatean Kingdom.

The Sunken City of Heracleion: Submerged off the coast of Egypt for over 1,200 years, the Sunken City of Heracleion was a bustling port city mentioned in ancient texts but long considered a myth. Its discovery in the early 2000s revealed a wealth of artifacts, including statues, temples, and ships, providing new insights into Egypt's maritime history and trade networks.

The Tomb of the Red Queen: Discovered within the ancient Maya city of Palenque in Mexico, the Tomb of the Red Queen contained the remains of a noblewoman adorned with jade jewelry and other precious offerings. The identity of the Red Queen and her significance within Maya society continue to puzzle archaeologists, offering tantalizing clues about the city's royal lineage and religious practices.

The Vinland Map: The Vinland Map, purportedly depicting the coastline of North America explored by Norse Vikings around the year 1000 CE, was hailed as a groundbreaking discovery when it surfaced in the 20th century. However, its authenticity has been hotly debated among scholars, with some claiming it to be a forgery crafted to support the idea of pre-Columbian transatlantic voyages.

The Dead Sea Scrolls

The discovery of the Dead Sea Scrolls in the caves of Qumran near the Dead Sea represents one of the most significant archaeological finds of the 20th century. Dating back over 2,000 years, these remarkably well-preserved manuscripts comprise a diverse collection of biblical texts, religious writings, and community regulations. Among the scrolls are fragments of every book of the Hebrew Bible except for the Book of Esther. Scholars have meticulously studied the Dead Sea Scrolls to decipher their contents and understand their historical context, revealing the beliefs, rituals, and sectarian divisions within Judaism at the time. Beyond their religious significance, the scrolls also provide valuable linguistic and textual evidence for understanding the development of the Hebrew language and biblical interpretation. Overall, the Dead Sea Scrolls continue to be a rich source of knowledge for researchers exploring the ancient world and the origins of Judaism.

The Hidden City of Machu Picchu: Built by the Inca Empire in the 15th century and hidden within the Andean mountains of Peru, Machu Picchu is a marvel of engineering and architecture. Abandoned and forgotten for centuries, it was rediscovered by explorer Hiram Bingham in 1911, revealing an intricate network of terraces, temples, and residential buildings.

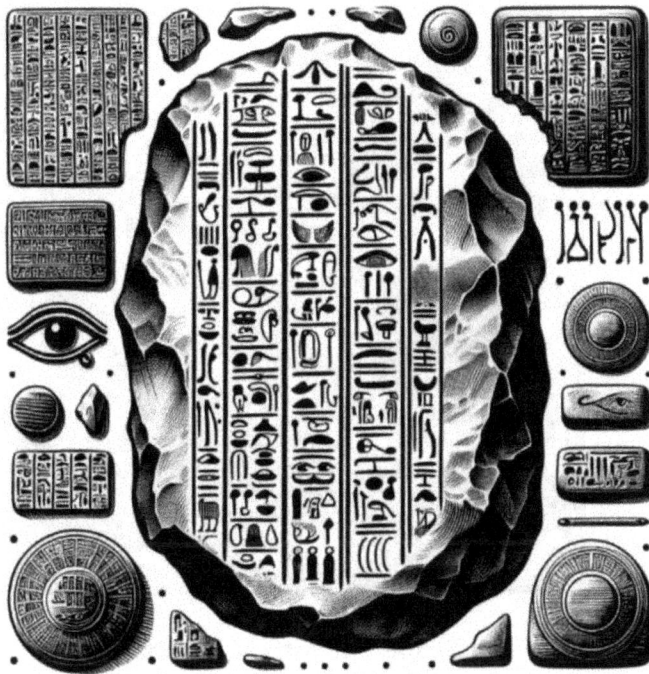

The Rosetta Stone

The discovery of the Rosetta Stone in Egypt in 1799 proved instrumental in deciphering ancient Egyptian hieroglyphs. The Rosetta Stone, with its inscriptions in multiple languages, including Greek, demotic, and hieroglyphs, served as a vital tool for linguists and scholars seeking to decode the enigmatic script of ancient Egypt. This breakthrough enabled the translation of countless other ancient Egyptian texts, opening a window into the rich history, literature, and religious beliefs of one of the world's oldest civilizations.

The Sumerian King List: The Sumerian King List, an ancient cuneiform tablet discovered in Mesopotamia, documents the reigns of Sumerian kings and dynasties dating back over 5,000 years. It provides valuable insights into early Mesopotamian history and mythology, including legendary rulers and their supposed reigns lasting thousands of years.

The Stone Spheres of Costa Rica

Scattered throughout the jungles of Costa Rica, the Stone Spheres of Disquis are a collection of perfectly spherical stone artifacts dating back over 1,000 years. Their purpose and significance remain a mystery, with theories ranging from astronomical markers to symbols of status and power within ancient indigenous societies.

The Tomb of the Sunken Skulls: Located in the ancient city of Chan in Peru, the Tomb of the Sunken Skulls contained the remains of over 100 individuals, including women and children. This archaeological find shed light on the religious beliefs and funerary practices of the Chimu civilization, who inhabited the region over 1,000 years ago.

The Tomb of Qin Shi Huang's Concubines

Excavated near the mausoleum of China's first Emperor, Qin Shi Huang, the Tomb of the Concubines contained the remains of over 100 women believed to have been sacrificed to accompany the emperor in the afterlife. This grim discovery sheds light on the brutal rituals and power dynamics of the Qin Dynasty, offering a glimpse into the lives of royal concubines in ancient China. The tomb offers a haunting insight into the dark rituals and hierarchical structures of ancient Chinese society. Within this somber burial site lay the remains of over a hundred women, likely chosen for their beauty and status, sacrificially interred to serve their emperor in the afterlife. Their tragic fate underscores the immense power wielded by rulers like Qin Shi Huang and highlights the profound sacrifices made by individuals in service to imperial ambitions. This grim discovery stands as a poignant reminder of the complexities and cruelties of dynastic China's royal courts.

Mysterious Ancient Civilizations

The Sunken City of Yonaguni: Off the coast of Japan's Yonaguni Island lies a submerged structure known as the Yonaguni Monument, consisting of massive stone blocks arranged in a geometric pattern. Discovered in 1986, the origins of the Yonaguni Monument remain a mystery, with theories ranging from natural geological formation to man-made construction, sparking debates among archaeologists and geologists.

The Enigmatic Purpose of Stonehenge: Stonehenge, a prehistoric monument in England composed of massive stone blocks arranged in concentric circles, continues to puzzle archaeologists with its enigmatic purpose. While theories abound, ranging from astronomical observatory to ceremonial site, the true function of Stonehenge remains a mystery, leaving scholars to speculate about its significance to ancient peoples.

The Hidden Chambers of the Great Pyramid: The Great Pyramid of Giza, one of the Seven Wonders of the Ancient World, continues to intrigue researchers with its hidden chambers and passageways. Despite centuries of exploration and speculation, the purpose of these chambers and their contents remain a mystery, inspiring theories about secret chambers, hidden treasures, and ancient mysteries.

The Mysterious Collapse of the Maya Civilization: The Maya civilization, known for its advanced mathematics, astronomy, and monumental architecture, experienced a mysterious collapse around the 9th century CE, leading to the abandonment of major cities and the decline of central authority. The reasons for the Maya collapse remain a subject of debate, with theories ranging from environmental degradation to social unrest and warfare.

The Elongated Skulls of Paracas

The Paracas culture of ancient Peru practiced artificial cranial deformation, resulting in elongated skulls that continue to fascinate researchers with their unusual shape and size. While some theories suggest that the practice was a form of social differentiation or ritualistic significance, the true purpose behind cranial deformation in Paracas society remains uncertain. Furthermore, recent genetic analysis of the Paracas skulls has sparked further intrigue, as some studies suggest that these individuals may have had genetic variations not found in typical Native American populations. This has led to speculation about possible genetic influences from other regions or even extraterrestrial origins, although these hypotheses remain speculative and controversial within the scientific community. Despite the mysteries surrounding the Paracas skulls, they serve as a tangible link to the ancient practices and beliefs of a civilization that thrived in the Peruvian desert thousands of years ago.

The Indus Valley Civilization's Disappearing Script: The ancient Indus Valley Civilization, known for its advanced urban planning and sophisticated sewage systems, developed a script that remains undeciphered to this day. Despite being one of the oldest writing systems in the world, scholars have been unable to decipher the Indus script, leading to speculation about its purpose and meaning.

The Olmec Colossal Heads: The Olmec civilization of ancient Mesoamerica created colossal stone heads weighing several tons each, featuring distinct facial features and headdresses. Despite their impressive craftsmanship, the purpose and significance of the Olmec colossal heads remain unknown, leading to speculation about their role in religious rituals or as representations of powerful rulers.

The Megalithic Temples of Malta: The Maltese archipelago is home to several megalithic temples, including the UNESCO World Heritage site of Ġgantija, dating back over 5,000 years. Despite their impressive construction and elaborate decorations, the purpose of these temples and the identity of their builders remain shrouded in mystery, adding to the allure of Malta's ancient past.

The Lost City of Cahokia: Cahokia, located near present-day St. Louis, Missouri, was once one of the largest cities in North America, inhabited by the Mississippian culture between the 9th and 15th centuries. Despite its size and influence, the reasons for Cahokia's decline and abandonment remain unclear, with theories ranging from environmental degradation to social upheaval.

The Unsolved Riddles of Teotihuacan: Teotihuacan, an ancient city located near present-day Mexico City, was one of the largest urban centers of the pre-Columbian Americas, yet its origins and decline remain shrouded in mystery. Despite its monumental pyramids and temples, the identity of Teotihuacan's founders and the reasons for its collapse remain elusive, fueling speculation about its role as a cosmopolitan hub and its eventual demise.

The Unexplained Megaliths of Gobekli Tepe

Gobekli Tepe's monumental stone pillars, adorned with intricate carvings of animals and symbols, suggest a sophisticated level of craftsmanship and communal effort. Some researchers speculate that Gobekli Tepe served as a ceremonial or ritualistic site, possibly for gatherings or religious ceremonies, indicating that organized social structures may have existed earlier than previously thought. The discovery of Gobekli Tepe has reshaped our understanding of prehistoric civilizations, suggesting that complex societies with advanced architectural skills may have emerged earlier in human history than previously believed. Despite ongoing excavations and research, many questions about Gobekli Tepe remain unanswered, adding to its allure as one of archaeology's most enigmatic sites.

The Lost Civilization of Atlantis: The legendary lost civilization of Atlantis, first described by the ancient Greek philosopher Plato, continues to capture the imagination with its tales of advanced technology and catastrophic destruction. While the existence of Atlantis remains unproven, the story of a prosperous civilization submerged beneath the sea continues to inspire speculation and exploration.

The Enigmatic Lines of the Amazon Rainforest: The Amazon rainforest is home to mysterious geometric earthworks known as geoglyphs, created by ancient civilizations between 200 BCE and 1283 CE. Despite their scale and intricacy, the purpose of these earthworks and the identity of their creators remain unknown, challenging conventional theories about pre-Columbian societies in the Amazon.

The Great Sphinx of Giza's Enigmatic Origins: The Great Sphinx of Giza, a colossal limestone statue with the body of a lion and the head of a human, continues to puzzle researchers with its mysterious origins and purpose. While commonly associated with the pharaoh Khafre, the identity of the Sphinx's builder and the reasons for its construction remain subjects of debate among Egyptologists.

The Underwater City of Dwarka: Dwarka, located off the coast of Gujarat, India, is said to be the legendary city of Lord Krishna, submerged beneath the Arabian Sea. While archaeological investigations have uncovered evidence of ancient structures and artifacts at Dwarka, the extent of its underwater ruins and the veracity of its legendary status remain subjects of debate.

The Puzzling Sacsayhuaman Walls: The ancient Inca fortress of Sacsayhuaman, located near Cusco, Peru, features massive stone walls composed of precisely cut and fitted blocks weighing up to 200 tons each. Despite the ingenuity of Inca engineering, the purpose behind the construction of Sacsayhuaman's walls and the techniques used to transport and shape the massive stones remain a mystery.

The Lost City of Mohenjo-Daro

Mohenjo-Daro, located in present-day Pakistan, was one of the largest cities of the ancient Indus Valley Civilization, yet its decline and abandonment around 1900 BCE remain shrouded in mystery. Mohenjo-Daro's urban planning and advanced infrastructure, including its grid layout and well-engineered sewage system, indicate a highly organized society with a keen understanding of city planning. However, archaeological evidence suggests that Mohenjo-Daro faced challenges such as flooding and declining trade routes, which may have contributed to its eventual demise. The absence of defensive structures and evidence of widespread destruction have led to speculation about possible causes, including natural disasters or conflicts with neighboring civilizations. Despite extensive excavations and research, the precise reasons for Mohenjo-Daro's decline remain speculative, fueling ongoing debates among archaeologists and historians about the fate of this ancient city.

Legends & Myths of Different Cultures

The Yara-Ma-Yha-Who of Aboriginal Australian Folklore: In Aboriginal Australian folklore, the Yara-Ma-Yha-Who is a diminutive, red-skinned creature with sucker-like hands and feet, said to lurk in fig trees and ambush unsuspecting travelers, draining their blood and swallowing them whole before regurgitating them later. Stories of the Yara-Ma-Yha-Who are used to teach children about the dangers of wandering alone in the bush and the importance of listening to their elders' advice.

The Drop Bear of Australian Folklore: In Australian folklore, the Drop Bear is a mythical creature resembling a large, predatory koala said to inhabit treetops and ambush unsuspecting travelers by dropping down from above. Tales of the Drop Bear serve as cautionary warnings to bushwalkers and campers, encouraging them to remain vigilant and avoid venturing into dense forested areas alone.

The Chupacabra of Latin American Legend: Across Latin America, the Chupacabra is a legendary creature said to roam the countryside, attacking livestock and draining their blood, leaving behind mysterious puncture wounds. Descriptions of the Chupacabra vary, with some likening it to a reptilian creature with spines or quills along its back, while others envision it as a hairless, kangaroo-like beast.

The Gashadokuro of Japanese Mythology: In Japanese mythology, the Gashadokuro is a gigantic skeleton monster formed from the bones of people who died of starvation or in battle, roaming the countryside at night and preying on lone travelers. Believed to be the vengeful spirits of the deceased, Gashadokuro are said to emit a distinctive rattling sound before attacking their victims. According to legend, the only way to repel or appease these monstrous beings is through rituals or offerings performed by Shinto priests, highlighting the cultural significance of spiritual practices in warding off malevolent forces.

The Kappa of Japanese Folklore

In Japanese folklore, the Kappa is a mischievous water-dwelling creature resembling a humanoid turtle, known for its love of cucumbers and habit of luring humans, particularly children, into bodies of water. Despite its playful demeanor, the Kappa is also feared for its strength and cunningness, leading to various protective charms and rituals to ward off its influence. The Kappa's origins date back centuries in Japanese folklore, where it is often depicted as both a trickster and a dangerous entity, inhabiting rivers, lakes, and ponds throughout the country. Tales of encounters with Kappas vary, with some stories portraying them as harmless pranksters while others describe them as malevolent creatures that drown unsuspecting victims. To protect against Kappa attacks, people would often carry cucumbers, believed to be the creature's favorite food, or bow deeply to show respect, as Kappas are known to return the gesture, spilling the water contained in the bowl-shaped depression on their heads and rendering them powerless. Despite its mythical nature, the legend of the Kappa continues to capture the imagination of Japanese culture, influencing art, literature, and popular media.

The Chupacabra of Latin American Legend: Across Latin America, the Chupacabra is a legendary creature said to roam the countryside, attacking livestock and draining their blood, leaving behind mysterious puncture wounds. Descriptions of the Chupacabra vary, with some likening it to a reptilian creature with spines or quills along its back, while others envision it as a hairless, kangaroo-like beast.

The Tokoloshe of Zulu Mythology: In Zulu mythology, the Tokoloshe is a malevolent water spirit or imp, often depicted as a small, grotesque humanoid creature with sharp teeth and glowing red eyes, capable of causing mischief and harm to those who cross its path. According to legend, the Tokoloshe can be summoned by witch doctors or used to enact revenge on enemies, instilling fear and superstition in local communities.

The Ninki Nanka of West African Folklore: Across West Africa, the Ninki Nanka is a legendary creature described as a massive, serpent-like beast with a horse's head and long neck, said to inhabit swamps and marshlands, where it preys on unsuspecting travelers. Stories of the Ninki Nanka serve as cautionary tales, warning against venturing into dangerous or unexplored territories, particularly at night.

The Grootslang of South African Mythology: In South African mythology, the Grootslang is a legendary creature said to inhabit deep caves and waterholes, possessing the body of an elephant and the tail of a serpent. According to legend, the Grootslang is immensely powerful and cunning, capable of luring unsuspecting victims into its lair to devour them.

The Yuki-Onna of Japanese Folklore: In Japanese folklore, the Yuki-Onna, or "Snow Woman," is a spirit associated with winter and snowstorms, appearing as a beautiful woman with icy blue skin and long black hair. According to legend, Yuki-Onna lures travelers astray in blizzards, freezing them with her breath or leading them to their demise in the snow.

The Mongolian Death Worm

In Mongolian folklore, the Mongolian Death Worm is a legendary creature said to inhabit the Gobi Desert, resembling a large, blood-red worm with deadly venom capable of spitting or electrocuting its prey from a distance. Despite numerous reported sightings and local beliefs in its existence, scientific evidence for the Mongolian Death Worm remains elusive. The legend of the Mongolian Death Worm has persisted for centuries among the nomadic tribes of the Gobi Desert, with many locals claiming to have encountered or witnessed the creature's deadly abilities. Descriptions of the worm vary, with some accounts depicting it as a massive, serpent-like creature capable of burrowing through sand and rock, while others describe it as a smaller, more worm-like entity. The mystery and intrigue surrounding the creature continues to captivate imaginations around the world, making it a fascinating subject of study and speculation in cryptozoology and popular culture alike.

The Manananggal of Philippine Mythology: In Philippine mythology, the Manananggal is a mythical creature resembling a beautiful woman by day but transforming into a hideous, bat-winged monster at night, capable of detaching its upper torso and flying to prey on pregnant women and unborn children. Tales of the Manananggal serve as cautionary warnings against infidelity and promiscuity, emphasizing the consequences of breaking societal norms.

The Aswang of Philippine Mythology: In Philippine mythology, the Aswang is a shape-shifting creature with vampiric tendencies, capable of transforming into various forms, including a bat, bird, or pig, to prey on humans, particularly pregnant women, and children. According to legend, the Aswang feeds on the flesh and blood of its victims under the cover of darkness, instilling fear and superstition in rural communities.

The Alux of Mayan Mythology: In Mayan mythology, the Alux is a mischievous spirit or dwarf believed to inhabit forests, caves, and ancient ruins, capable of both helping and harming humans depending on their behavior. According to legend, offerings of food and drink are made to appease the Alux and seek their protection, particularly by farmers and travelers. Described as a diminutive creature, the Alux is believed to possess magical powers and the ability to shape-shift, often appearing as a child or an animal to interact with humans. While Aluxob (plural form of Alux) are generally mischievous and playful, they can also be capricious and unpredictable, sometimes causing mischief or leading travelers astray in the wilderness. Despite their mischievous nature, the Alux is also revered as guardians of the natural world, and offerings such as corn, honey, or tobacco are made to them to ensure their benevolence and protection. The belief in Aluxob remains deeply ingrained in Mayan culture, influencing rituals, superstitions, and traditional practices to this day.

he Bunyip of Australian Aboriginal Mythology: In Australian Aboriginal mythology, the Bunyip is a mythical creature believed to inhabit waterholes and swamps, described as a large, amphibious monster with various features such as a dog-like face, long neck, and sharp claws. While sightings and folklore surrounding the Bunyip persist to this day, its exact nature and origins remain shrouded in mystery.

The Vegetable Lamb of Tartary: In medieval European folklore, the Vegetable Lamb of Tartary is a mythical creature believed to grow from a plant resembling a lamb tethered to the earth by its stem. According to legend, the lamb feeds on the surrounding vegetation until it devours all within reach, at which point it perishes, and its wool can be harvested to make fabric.

The Hodag of American Folklore: In American folklore, the Hodag is a mythical creature said to inhabit the forests of Wisconsin, resembling a fearsome combination of a bull, dinosaur, and lizard, with horns, spikes, and sharp teeth. Despite its origins as a hoax created by a local prankster in the 19th century, the legend of the Hodag persists as a popular symbol of Wisconsin folklore and tourism.

The Jiangshi of Chinese Folklore: In Chinese folklore, the Jiangshi, or "hopping vampire," is a reanimated corpse that hops or floats along the ground, preying on the living to absorb their life force or qi. According to legend, Jiangshi are created through improper burial rites or the influence of malevolent spirits, and they can be repelled or destroyed using Taoist magic or rituals.

The Dobhar-Chú of Irish Mythology: In Irish folklore, the Dobhar-Chú is a mythical creature resembling a giant otter or dog with a vicious temper and a fondness for freshwater lakes and rivers. According to legend, the Dobhar-Chú is known for its deadly attacks on humans, particularly those who venture too close to its territory or disturb its offspring. Despite its fearsome reputation, tales of encounters with the Dobhar-Chú continue to captivate imaginations in Irish folklore, with some attributing its existence to sightings of large marine creatures or mysterious water-dwelling animals.

The Golem of Jewish Folklore

In Jewish folklore, the Golem is a humanoid creature made from clay or mud and brought to life through mystical rituals, often to serve as a protector or defender of the Jewish community. According to legend, the Golem possesses great strength but lacks free will, requiring a specific command to animate or deactivate it. The concept of the Golem originated from Jewish folklore, particularly in the mystical traditions of Kabbalah, where it symbolizes humanity's capacity for creation and the ethical implications of playing God. According to legend, the Golem was created by a learned rabbi or wise man who inscribed sacred Hebrew words onto its forehead, imbuing it with life. However, the Golem's power was also its limitation, as it could easily become uncontrollable and wreak havoc if not properly commanded or controlled. Tales of the Golem have been passed down through generations, reflecting themes of power, responsibility, and the consequences of meddling with forces beyond human understanding. Despite its mythical origins, the Golem continues to capture the imagination of storytellers and scholars alike, serving as a symbol of the supernatural and the boundaries between life and death in Jewish folklore.

The Thunderbird of Native American Legend

The Thunderbird holds a significant place in the mythology and spiritual beliefs of various Native American tribes across North America. It is often depicted as a majestic bird with feathers resembling lightning bolts and eyes that flash like lightning itself. Legends describe the Thunderbird as a creature of immense power, capable of creating thunder with the flapping of its wings and generating lightning with the blink of its eyes. Additionally, the Thunderbird is often associated with supernatural feats and acts of heroism, representing the forces of nature and the spiritual connection between humans and the natural world. The Thunderbird's presence in Native American folklore serves as a reminder of the deep reverence and respect indigenous cultures hold for the land, the elements, and the mysteries of the universe.

Forgotten Histories of Empires

The Kingdom of Aksum's Naval Expedition: The Aksumite Empire, centered in present-day Ethiopia, once launched a naval expedition to the Roman-controlled Red Sea, intending to capture the Roman port of Adulis. Despite initial success, the Aksumite fleet ultimately faced defeat when the Roman navy retaliated, highlighting the empire's ambitious maritime ventures.

The Kangaba War and the Mali Empire: In the 13th century, the Mali Empire faced internal strife known as the Kangaba War, where the Sosso Kingdom attempted to conquer Mali. What's unusual is that during the decisive battle, the Mali forces, led by Sundiata Keita, utilized a magic object called the "Gbara," believed to possess mystical powers that ensured victory, solidifying Sundiata's reign as the first emperor of Mali.

The Inca Empire's Road System: The Inca Empire of pre-Columbian South America constructed an extensive network of roads spanning thousands of kilometers across the Andes Mountains, connecting distant provinces and facilitating communication, trade, and imperial control. These roads, built with remarkable engineering skill using stone blocks and featuring suspension bridges and staircases, enabled the efficient movement of goods, troops, and messengers, contributing to the cohesion and resilience of the Inca state.

The Aztec Empire's Floating Gardens: The Aztec Empire of ancient Mexico built innovative floating gardens called "chinampas" in the shallow waters of Lake Texcoco, allowing them to cultivate crops and sustain large populations in the arid environment of the Valley of Mexico. These artificial islands were constructed by layering mud and vegetation, providing fertile land for agriculture, and showcasing the empire's advanced engineering and agricultural techniques.

The Kingdom of Kush's Pyramids: While ancient Egypt is renowned for its pyramids, fewer people are aware that the Kingdom of Kush, located in present-day Sudan, also constructed its own pyramids as symbols of royal power and religious significance. The Kushite pyramids, built at sites like Meroe and Nuri, exhibit unique architectural features and burial practices distinct from their Egyptian counterparts, reflecting the cultural and political influence of Kush in the Nile Valley.

The Delian League's Tribute Lists: The Delian League, an alliance of Greek city-states led by Athens during the 5th century BCE, maintained detailed tribute lists documenting the contributions of member states in the form of monetary payments and resources. These lists provide valuable insights into the economic and political dynamics of ancient Greece, revealing patterns of dominance, resistance, and cooperation within the league.

The Kingdom of Axum's Christian Legacy: The Kingdom of Axum, located in present-day Ethiopia and Eritrea, was one of the first states to officially adopt Christianity as the state religion in the 4th century CE, preceding the conversion of the Roman Empire. Axum's Christian legacy, evidenced by iconic structures like the Church of St. Mary of Zion and the Ezana Stone inscriptions, played a pivotal role in shaping the religious and cultural landscape of the region.

The Kingdom of Axum's Maritime Trade: The Kingdom of Axum, situated along the Red Sea coast, was a major maritime power in the ancient world, engaging in extensive trade with distant lands such as India, Egypt, and the Arabian Peninsula. Axum's control over strategic ports like Adulis allowed it to dominate sea routes and prosper from lucrative trade networks, shaping its economy and cultural exchanges with foreign civilizations.

The Mughal Empire's Elephant Tactics

During the Mughal Empire's expansion into South India, Emperor Akbar employed a unique tactic using war elephants outfitted with blades on their tusks to break the enemy's ranks and sow chaos on the battlefield. As the Mughal forces charged into battle atop these formidable creatures, the sight of razor-sharp tusks struck terror into the hearts of their opponents. The elephants, trained to charge and trample through enemy lines, unleashed devastation. Recognizing the psychological impact and physical prowess of war elephants in battle, Akbar's ingenious use of war elephants with bladed tusks showcased his strategic acumen and contributed to the expansion and consolidation of Mughal power in the region.

The Maurya Empire's Edicts: The Maurya Empire of ancient India, under the reign of Emperor Ashoka, issued a series of edicts carved on pillars and rock surfaces throughout the empire, promoting principles of Buddhist ethics, tolerance, and social welfare. These edicts, written in various regional languages and scripts, served as public declarations of Ashoka's policies and beliefs, exerting a profound influence on the religious and moral life of Mauryan society.

The Maratha Empire's Guerrilla Warfare: The Maratha Empire in India, known for its resistance against Mughal and British rule, employed guerrilla warfare tactics known as "ganimi kava" to harass and weaken enemy forces through hit-and-run attacks, ambushes, and raids. Led by skilled commanders like Shivaji Maharaj, the Marathas utilized their knowledge of the terrain and agile cavalry to outmaneuver larger armies, demonstrating the effectiveness of asymmetrical warfare against superior adversaries.

The Yuan Dynasty's Paper Currency: During the Yuan Dynasty in China, founded by Kublai Khan, the empire introduced paper currency known as "chao" or "xiaochao," becoming one of the first governments in the world to issue fiat money backed by the state. This innovative monetary system facilitated trade and economic development within the vast empire, but also faced challenges such as inflation and counterfeiting, highlighting the complexities of early financial systems.

The Byzantine Empire's Greek Fire: The Byzantine Empire developed Greek Fire, a highly flammable liquid weapon used in naval warfare, capable of burning on water and causing devastation to enemy ships. The exact composition of Greek Fire, a closely guarded secret, remains a mystery to this day, but its effectiveness in repelling Arab and Viking fleets played a crucial role in Byzantine naval supremacy and defense of Constantinople.

The Khmer Empire's Hydraulic Engineering: The Khmer Empire, centered in present-day Cambodia, was renowned for its advanced hydraulic engineering and water management systems, including elaborate reservoirs, canals, and rice paddies, such as the iconic Angkor Wat complex. These engineering feats enabled the Khmer to harness the monsoon rains and sustain large urban populations, supporting the empire's economic prosperity and cultural achievements during its zenith.

The Inca Empire's Quipu

The Inca Empire of pre-Columbian South America utilized a unique system of knotted cords called quipu to record numerical and narrative information, serving as a form of communication, record-keeping, and administration. While quipus were primarily used for accounting and census purposes, recent research suggests they may have also conveyed complex messages and stories through the arrangement and color-coding of knots, representing an indigenous form of writing and storytelling.

The Hittite Empire's Peace Treaty: The Hittite Empire, based in Anatolia during the Late Bronze Age, is known for its diplomatic prowess, exemplified by the earliest recorded peace treaty in history, the Treaty of Kadesh. This treaty, concluded between the Hittite king Hattusili III and the Egyptian pharaoh Ramses II around 1258 BCE, ended decades of conflict between the two powers and established a lasting peace, demonstrating the effectiveness of diplomacy in ancient international relations.

The Parthian Empire's Cataphracts: The Parthian Empire, a powerful Iranian civilization that rivaled Rome, fielded heavily armored cavalry units known as cataphracts, equipped with lances, bows, and armored horses, capable of charging enemy lines with devastating force. Parthian cataphracts, renowned for their discipline and mobility, played a crucial role in battles against Roman legions and other adversaries, demonstrating the effectiveness of shock cavalry tactics in ancient warfare.

The Moche Empire's Elaborate Tombs

The Moche civilization of ancient Peru constructed elaborate tombs for their elite rulers and priests, featuring intricate murals, pottery, and precious artifacts depicting scenes of ritual sacrifice, warfare, and daily life. These tombs served as religious and ceremonial centers, preserving Moche culture and beliefs for future generations, and providing valuable insights into their social hierarchy and religious practices.

Mythological Tales Around the World

The Feathered Serpent Quetzalcoatl: In Aztec mythology, Quetzalcoatl was a feathered serpent deity associated with wind, fertility, and creation. Legend has it that Quetzalcoatl was banished from the underworld and vowed to return, leading to the belief that the Spanish conquistador Hernán Cortés was the deity's prophesied return, contributing to the fall of the Aztec empire.

The Norse Goddess Gefjun and the Creation of Zealand: According to Norse mythology, the goddess Gefjun plowed the land of Sweden with four oxen and created the island of Zealand in Denmark. To thank her, the king promised Gefjun as much land as she could plow in one night, leading her to transform her four sons into powerful oxen and carve out Zealand from the Swedish mainland.

The Australian Dreamtime: In Aboriginal Australian mythology, the Dreamtime, or "the Dreaming," is a sacred era when ancestral spirits created the world and its inhabitants. Dreamtime stories explain the origins of the land, animals, plants, and natural phenomena, shaping Aboriginal cultural beliefs, laws, and traditions for thousands of years.

The Japanese Sun Goddess Amaterasu: Amaterasu is the Shinto goddess of the sun and the universe in Japanese mythology, revered as the ancestor of the imperial family. According to legend, Amaterasu withdrew into a cave in protest, plunging the world into darkness, until she was lured out by a clever ruse involving a mirror and a sacred dance.

The Chinese Dragon Kings: In Chinese mythology, there are four Dragon Kings who rule over the four seas and are responsible for controlling the weather and the tides. Each Dragon King has a distinct personality and appearance, with legends often portraying them as powerful and wise rulers capable of both benevolence and wrath.

The Trickster Figure Anansi

Anansi the spider is a prominent figure in West African and Caribbean folklore, known as a trickster and storyteller. In one tale, Anansi outwits the sky god Nyame to gain control of all stories, demonstrating his cunning and resourcefulness in overcoming challenges.

The Greek Sphinx Riddle: The Sphinx, a creature with the body of a lion and the head of a human, is famous in Greek mythology for posing a riddle to travelers and devouring those who could not answer correctly. The riddle, "What walks on four legs in the morning, two legs at noon, and three legs in the evening?" was eventually solved by Oedipus, who answered, "Man, who crawls on all fours as a baby, walks on two legs as an adult, and uses a cane in old age."

The Egyptian Goddess Bastet: Bastet, the Egyptian goddess of home, fertility, and domesticity, was often depicted as a lioness or as a woman with the head of a lioness. Despite her benevolent nature, Bastet was also associated with warfare and protection, serving as both a nurturing mother figure and a fierce guardian of her devotees.

The Mayan Hero Twins

According to Mayan mythology, the Hero Twins, Hunahpu and Xbalanque, embarked on a series of epic adventures and trials to overcome the lords of the underworld and avenge their father's death. Through cunning and bravery, the twins outsmarted their enemies and emerged victorious, becoming symbols of resilience and triumph in Mayan culture.

The Finnish Kalevala Epic: The Kalevala is a Finnish national epic that recounts the mythic origins of the world, featuring heroes, gods, and magical creatures. One of the most famous tales from the Kalevala is the story of the creation of the Sampo, a mystical artifact that brings prosperity and abundance to its possessor.

The Slavic Domovoi House Spirit: In Slavic folklore, the domovoi is a household spirit that protects the home and its inhabitants but can also play mischievous tricks if not respected. Domovoi are believed to reside in the hearth or under the threshold and are appeased with offerings of food, drink, and kindness from the household occupants.

The Polynesian Demigod Maui: Maui is a legendary figure in Polynesian mythology, known as a trickster and hero who performed great feats to benefit humanity. One of Maui's most famous exploits was the theft of fire from the underworld, which he snatched from the jaws of the fire goddess Mahuika, bringing warmth and light to the world.

The Hindu Monkey God Hanuman: Hanuman is a central figure in Hindu mythology, revered as the loyal devotee of the god Rama and a symbol of strength, devotion, and service. Hanuman is depicted as a monkey with supernatural powers, capable of flight and transformation, and is worshiped by millions of Hindus around the world.

The Amazonian Yara-Ma-Yha-Who: The Yara-Ma-Yha-Who is a mythical creature from Aboriginal Australian and Amazonian folklore, described as a small, red-skinned humanoid with a large head and mouth. According to legend, the Yara-Ma-Yha-Who lurks in trees and ambushes unsuspecting travelers, draining their blood with its sucker-like fingers before swallowing them whole and regurgitating them as its minions.

The Aboriginal Rainbow Serpent

In Aboriginal Australian mythology, the Rainbow Serpent, also known as the Rainbow Snake or Rainbow Dreaming, is a fundamental creator deity and an embodiment of profound spiritual significance. Revered across various Aboriginal cultures, the Rainbow Serpent is believed to possess immense power, shaping the land, and influencing the natural world through its movements. According to Dreamtime narratives, the Rainbow Serpent's journey traversed vast distances, carving out valleys, gorges, and waterways, which are seen as sacred sites by Indigenous communities. The Rainbow Serpent's association with water underscores its role as a custodian of life and fertility, symbolizing the essential link between water, sustenance, and spiritual renewal. Its presence in Aboriginal art, rituals, and storytelling reflects the deep cultural connection to the land and the enduring spiritual traditions passed down through generations.

The Hawaiian Goddess Pele: Pele is the Hawaiian goddess of fire, lightning, wind, and volcanoes, revered as both a creator and destroyer of land. According to legend, Pele resides in the Halemaʻumaʻu crater at the summit of Kīlauea volcano on the island of Hawaiʻi, where she fiercely guards her domain and shapes the volcanic landscape with her fiery temper.

The Inuit Sea Goddess Sedna: Sedna is a powerful sea goddess in Inuit mythology, believed to reside at the bottom of the ocean and control the creatures of the sea. According to legend, Sedna's fingers became the first seals, whales, and other marine animals after she was cast into the sea by her father, demonstrating her transformative and creative powers.

The Persian Simurgh Bird: The Simurgh is a mythical bird from Persian mythology, often depicted as a majestic and benevolent creature with the head of a dog, the body of a lion, and the wings of an eagle. According to legend, the Simurgh possesses profound wisdom and knowledge, serving as a guide and protector to those who seek enlightenment.

The Celtic Goddess Morrigan: Morrigan is a complex and enigmatic figure in Celtic mythology, often depicted as a goddess of war, fate, and sovereignty. She is associated with crows and ravens, which are believed to be her messengers, and is said to appear on the battlefield to foretell the outcome of conflicts and choose who will live or die.

The Tanuki: In Japanese mythology, the Tanuki is a mischievous shape-shifting creature resembling a raccoon dog, known for its playful and deceptive nature. According to folklore, the Tanuki possesses magical abilities, such as transforming leaves into gold coins or disguising themselves as humans or objects. Despite their trickster reputation, Tanuki are also revered as symbols of prosperity and good fortune in Japanese culture.

The Scottish Kelpie Water Horse

In Scottish folklore, the Kelpie emerges from the misty depths of lochs and rivers as a menacing yet captivating figure, weaving its dark allure into the tapestry of local legends. With its bewitching guise, the Kelpie lures unsuspecting travelers, drawn by the promise of a friendly encounter or a swift ride on its back. However, beneath its facade of charm lies a sinister intent, as the Kelpie seizes its victims with relentless force, dragging them into the icy embrace of the water. The creature's shapeshifting abilities add to its mystique, allowing it to assume various forms to suit its purposes, whether as a beguiling stranger or a magnificent equine steed. Its hooves, said to point backward, serve as a telltale sign of its otherworldly nature, instilling fear and awe in those who dare to gaze upon it. Yet, amidst its malevolence, whispers persist of Kelpie's dual nature, hinting at a potential for redemption or appeasement. Some tales speak of offerings made to the creature, tokens of reverence that may placate its wrath or even earn its protection. Thus, the legend of the Kelpie endures as a cautionary tale of the perilous waters, where beauty and danger converge in the enigmatic depths of Scottish folklore.

Intriguing Unsolved Mysteries

The Tamam Shud Case: Also known as the Mystery of the Somerton Man, this unsolved case involves the discovery of an unidentified man found dead on Somerton Beach in Australia in 1948, with a torn-out page from a book of Persian poetry containing the words "Tamam Shud" (meaning "ended" or "finished") found in his pocket. Despite extensive investigations and forensic analysis, the man's identity and cause of death remain unknown, fueling theories of espionage, foul play, or occult involvement.

The Bermuda Triangle: The Bermuda Triangle, a region of the North Atlantic Ocean infamous for the purported disappearance of ships and aircraft under mysterious circumstances, has captivated the public imagination for decades. Despite numerous theories ranging from magnetic anomalies to extraterrestrial activity, no conclusive evidence has been found to explain the disappearances, leaving the phenomenon shrouded in mystery.

The Taos Hum: Residents of Taos, New Mexico, have reported hearing a low-frequency humming sound known as the "Taos Hum" since the early 1990s, despite efforts by scientists and investigators to identify its source. The origin of the hum remains elusive, with theories ranging from industrial machinery and atmospheric disturbances to psychological phenomena, leaving residents and researchers alike puzzled by its persistence.

The Circleville Letters: Throughout the 1970s, residents of Circleville, Ohio, received anonymous letters containing threats, accusations, and personal information, leading to widespread fear and speculation within the community. Despite investigations and surveillance efforts, the identity of the Circleville Letter Writer remains unknown, fueling rumors of conspiracy, cover-up, and potential foul play.

The Sailing Stones of Death Valley

In California's Death Valley, large rocks weighing up to hundreds of kilograms mysteriously move across the desert floor, leaving long trails behind them, despite the absence of human or animal intervention. Despite scientific scrutiny and experiments, the mechanism behind the movement of the sailing stones remains a subject of debate, with theories ranging from strong winds and ice floes to magnetic fields and geological phenomena.

The Toynbee Tiles: Since the 1980s, cryptic messages known as the Toynbee Tiles have appeared embedded in asphalt streets across the United States and South America, bearing inscriptions such as "Toynbee Idea in Movie 2001 Resurrect Dead on Planet Jupiter" and "You Must Make + Glue Tiles!" Despite efforts to track down the creator or creators of the tiles, their identity and purpose remain unknown, sparking speculation about conspiracy theories, art projects, or cryptic messages from beyond.

The Dyatlov Pass Incident: In 1959, a group of experienced hikers died under mysterious circumstances in the Ural Mountains of Russia, with evidence suggesting they tore their tents from the inside and fled barefoot into the freezing wilderness, leaving behind cryptic clues and injuries consistent with a high-speed impact. Despite multiple investigations and theories ranging from avalanches and hypothermia to military experiments and paranormal activity, the true cause of the Dyatlov Pass Incident remains unknown.

The Disappearance of Frederick Valentich: In 1978, Australian pilot Frederick Valentich disappeared while flying over the Bass Strait, reporting to air traffic control that he was being followed by an unidentified flying object before vanishing without a trace. Despite extensive search efforts, neither Valentich nor his plane were ever found, leaving investigators puzzled by the circumstances of his disappearance and the veracity of his UFO sighting.

The Green Children of Woolpit: In the 12th century, two children with green skin and unusual clothing reportedly emerged from a pit in the village of Woolpit, England, speaking an unknown language and displaying aversion to normal food. Despite attempts to integrate them into society, the children eventually lost their green color and adapted to their surroundings, leaving historians and folklorists puzzled by their origins and identity.

The Zodiac Killer: The Zodiac Killer is a notorious unidentified serial killer who operated in Northern California during the late 1960s and early 1970s, taunting law enforcement and the media with cryptic letters and ciphers. Despite extensive investigations and numerous suspects, the Zodiac Killer's identity remains unknown, with the case remaining one of the most infamous unsolved mysteries in American criminal history.

The Disappearance of Flight MH370: In 2014, Malaysia Airlines Flight MH370 vanished from radar screens during a routine flight from Kuala Lumpur to Beijing, with 239 passengers and crew on board. Despite an extensive multinational search effort, the wreckage of the plane has never been found, leaving investigators and aviation experts baffled by the circumstances of its disappearance and the fate of those on board.

The Lead Masks Case: In 1966, the bodies of two Brazilian electronic technicians were discovered on a hillside near Rio de Janeiro, wearing matching lead masks and with a notebook containing cryptic instructions and references to extraterrestrial contact. Despite extensive investigations, the true purpose of the lead masks and the circumstances of the men's deaths remain a mystery, with theories ranging from suicide cults to government experiments.

The Dyatlov Pass Incident: In 1959, a group of experienced hikers died under mysterious circumstances in the Ural Mountains of Russia, with evidence suggesting they tore their tents from the inside and fled barefoot into the freezing wilderness, leaving behind cryptic clues and injuries consistent with a high-speed impact. Despite multiple investigations and theories ranging from avalanches and hypothermia to military experiments and paranormal activity, the true cause of the Dyatlov Pass Incident remains unknown.

The Disappearance of the Mary Celeste Crew: In 1872, the crew of the merchant ship Mary Celeste was discovered missing in the Atlantic Ocean, with no sign of struggle or foul play and all personal belongings, valuables, and provisions left intact. Despite subsequent investigations and theories ranging from mutiny and piracy to paranormal activity the enduring allure of the mystery continues to beckon, drawing adventurers and storytellers into its embrace, where the line between fact and fiction blurs, and the enigma of the Mary Celeste lives on as a testament to the enduring fascination of maritime lore.

The Tunguska Event

In 1908, a massive explosion occurred near the Tunguska River in Siberia, flattening an estimated 80 million trees over an area of 2,000 square kilometers. Despite extensive scientific investigation, the cause of the explosion remains a subject of debate, with theories ranging from a meteorite impact and comet fragments to a natural gas explosion or even extraterrestrial intervention. Numerous eyewitness reports described a bright flash of light followed by a shockwave that knocked people off their feet hundreds of kilometers away, leading to speculation about the event's extraterrestrial origins. The Tunguska event is considered one of the most powerful atmospheric explosions in recorded history, releasing an estimated energy equivalent to 10–15 megatons of TNT, but leaving no impact crater, adding to the mystery surrounding its cause.

Incredible Natural Phenomena

Catatumbo Lightning

The Catatumbo Lightning phenomenon is a continuous display of lightning storms that occurs over Lake Maracaibo in Venezuela, particularly during the night. The lightning is caused by a unique combination of warm trade winds colliding with cool air masses over the lake, creating a perfect environment for the formation of electrical storms. Locally known as the "Relámpago del Catatumbo" or the "Everlasting Storm," this natural spectacle can produce up to 280 lightning flashes per hour, illuminating the night sky for hours on end. The Catatumbo Lightning has become a cultural symbol of the region and is even credited with aiding in the defense against invading forces throughout history, as the continuous lightning provided a natural warning system.

Penitentes: Penitentes are tall, thin blades of hardened snow or ice that form in high-altitude regions like the Andes. These eerie formations resemble fields of icy spires and are created through a combination of sunlight, sublimation (the transition of ice directly to vapor), and wind erosion, resulting in stunning and otherworldly landscapes.

Brinicles: Brinicles, also known as "ice stalactites" or "ice fingers," form beneath sea ice when cold, salty water sinks and freezes into a downward-growing icicle. These underwater ice formations create an otherworldly spectacle as they slowly descend towards the ocean floor, enveloping marine life in a delicate frozen sheath.

Sundogs: Sundogs, or parhelia, are bright spots that appear on either side of the sun and are caused by the refraction of sunlight through hexagonal ice crystals in the atmosphere. These dazzling optical illusions create the appearance of additional suns flanking the real sun and are often accompanied by vibrant halos and arcs.

Green Flash: The green flash is a rare optical phenomenon that occurs during sunrise or sunset when a green spot is briefly visible on the horizon. This fleeting phenomenon is caused by the refraction of sunlight through the Earth's atmosphere, with the green color resulting from the separation of light into its different wavelengths.

Bioluminescent Waves: Bioluminescent waves occur in various locations around the world, such as the Maldives and Vaadhoo Island, where microscopic organisms like phytoplankton or bioluminescent bacteria emit light when disturbed, creating mesmerizing glowing patterns in the water at night.

Fire Rainbows: Fire rainbows, or circumhorizontal arcs, are optical phenomena that occur when sunlight passes through hexagon-shaped ice crystals high in the atmosphere, refracting and dispersing light to create vibrant rainbow-like arcs that appear to set the sky ablaze with color.

Lenticular Clouds

Lenticular clouds are lens-shaped formations that typically form over mountain ranges and are caused by standing waves in the atmosphere. The stationary clouds are often mistaken for UFOs due to their unusual appearance and can appear stacked in layers or arranged in a stacked formation resembling a stack of pancakes.

Blue Lava: The blue lava of Indonesia's Kawah Ijen volcano emits an otherworldly blue glow at night due to the combustion of sulfuric gases. As molten sulfur flows from the crater and cools, it turns from red to orange to blue, creating a mesmerizing spectacle that attracts adventurous travelers from around the world.

Mammatus Clouds: Mammatus clouds are pouch-like formations that hang from the underside of storm clouds, often associated with severe thunderstorms. These ominous clouds are created by sinking air within the storm system and are characterized by their distinctive appearance, resembling a field of cotton balls or bubble wrap suspended in the sky.

Snow Rollers: Snow rollers are rare natural phenomena that occur under precise conditions of wind and temperature, resulting in the formation of cylindrical snowballs that roll across the landscape. These perfectly formed snow tubes are created when loose snow is blown by the wind and accumulates additional layers, creating a trail of rolling snow cylinders.

Volcanic Lightning: Volcanic lightning occurs during volcanic eruptions when static electricity is generated within the ash plumes as particles collide and interact. These dramatic displays of electrical activity illuminate the volcanic plume with flashes of lightning, creating a surreal and awe-inspiring spectacle amidst the eruptive chaos.

St. Elmo's Fire: St. Elmo's Fire is a natural atmospheric phenomenon that occurs during thunderstorms when a coronal discharge forms around pointed objects, such as ship masts or airplane wings. This electrical phenomenon creates a blue or violet glow resembling flames, often observed during storms at sea or in mountainous regions.

Morning Glory Clouds: Morning Glory Clouds are a rare meteorological phenomenon consisting of long, tubular cloud formations that can stretch for hundreds of kilometers. These unique clouds occur in specific regions, such as the Gulf of Carpentaria in Australia, and are often accompanied by powerful atmospheric waves that create ideal conditions for glider pilots seeking to ride the rolling tubes of clouds.

Moonbows: Moonbows, also known as lunar rainbows, are rainbow-like arcs that occur at night when moonlight is reflected and dispersed by water droplets in the atmosphere. These ethereal phenomena are less bright and vivid than traditional rainbows but create a faint yet enchanting arc of colors against the dark night sky.

Magnetic Termite Mounds

Magnetic termite mounds, found predominantly in northern Australia, are fascinating structures crafted by the tiny architects of the insect world. These mounds stand tall and thin, resembling ancient skyscrapers, with a distinct north-south orientation. What makes them even more remarkable is their ability to regulate temperature and humidity within the termite colony. Scientists believe that these mounds are aligned with Earth's magnetic field, which aids the termites in navigating their environment, though the precise mechanism behind this alignment remains a subject of ongoing research and fascination.

Supercells: Supercells are massive, rotating thunderstorms that are known for their severe weather and ability to produce tornadoes, large hail, and intense winds. These powerful storm systems are characterized by a rotating updraft known as a mesocyclone, which can sustain the storm for long periods and produce extreme weather conditions.

Red Tides: Red tides are caused by blooms of algae that produce toxins harmful to marine life, often leading to massive fish kills and discoloration of coastal waters. Some species of bioluminescent algae can also cause the ocean to glow red at night, creating a stunning yet potentially harmful natural phenomenon.

Frost Flowers

Frost flowers are delicate ice structures that form on the surface of plants under specific conditions of temperature and humidity. These intricate crystalline formations occur when water vapor in the air freezes directly onto the surface of vegetation, creating exquisite frozen blooms that shimmer in the morning light.

Supernatural & Paranormal Phenomena

The Curse of the Hope Diamond: The Hope Diamond, a famous gemstone with a storied history, is said to be cursed, bringing misfortune and tragedy to its owners. Legends surrounding the diamond include tales of suicides, accidents, and financial ruin, fueling beliefs in its supernatural powers of destruction.

The Dyatlov Pass Incident: In 1959, a group of experienced hikers died under mysterious circumstances in the Ural Mountains of Russia, in an event known as the Dyatlov Pass Incident. The hikers' tent was found torn from the inside, and their bodies exhibited unexplained injuries, leading to speculation about supernatural forces or government cover-ups.

Spontaneous Human Combustion

Spontaneous human combustion is a phenomenon where a person seemingly bursts into flames without an external heat source. Despite numerous documented cases throughout history, the cause remains unknown, leading to speculation about the paranormal.

The Philadelphia Experiment: The Philadelphia Experiment allegedly involved a covert U.S. Navy project in the 1940s aimed at rendering a warship invisible to radar using electromagnetic fields. Reports of bizarre phenomena, including time travel, teleportation, and crew members embedded in the ship's hull, have fueled speculation about the experiment's supernatural implications.

The Winchester Mystery House: The Winchester Mystery House in California is a sprawling mansion known for its labyrinthine layout and architectural oddities, allegedly built by Sarah Winchester, heiress to the Winchester rifle fortune, to appease vengeful spirits. The house features staircases that lead to nowhere, doors that open onto walls, and hidden passages, inspiring theories about supernatural influences guiding its construction.

The Curse of Tutankhamun's Tomb: The discovery of the tomb of Tutankhamun in 1922 by Howard Carter and Lord Carnarvon was followed by a series of mysterious deaths and accidents among those involved, leading to rumors of a curse associated with the ancient Egyptian pharaoh. Despite scientific explanations for the deaths, the curse of Tutankhamun's tomb remains a popular legend in paranormal lore.

The Stone Tape Theory: The Stone Tape Theory proposes that inanimate materials, such as stone or buildings, can absorb and retain energy from past events, leading to residual hauntings or ghostly manifestations. This theory attempts to explain why certain locations seem to replay past events like a recording.

The Hessdalen Lights: The Hessdalen lights are unexplained phenomena observed in the Hessdalen valley of Norway, consisting of glowing orbs or lights that appear in the sky and move in seemingly intelligent patterns. Despite extensive scientific study, the origin of the lights remains unknown, leading to speculation about UFOs, plasma phenomena, or other paranormal explanations.

The Devil's Footprints

In 1855, mysterious hoof-like tracks appeared overnight in the snow across rural England, covering vast distances and crossing obstacles such as rivers and rooftops. The phenomenon, known as the Devil's footprints, sparked fear and speculation about supernatural or diabolical origins, with various theories proposed to explain the bizarre tracks.

The Curse of the Crying Boy Paintings: In the 1980s, reports emerged of a series of paintings depicting crying boys, which were said to survive house fires unscathed while causing fires to spread elsewhere. Despite skepticism, the legend of the cursed paintings gained traction, leading to widespread fear and superstition surrounding the artwork.

The Curse of the Ouija Board: Ouija boards, used for divination and spirit communication, have long been associated with mysterious and sometimes sinister phenomena. Stories abound of individuals experiencing hauntings, possession, or other supernatural encounters after using the Ouija board, fueling beliefs in its ability to summon malevolent spirits or open portals to other dimensions.

The Devil's Tramping Ground: The Devil's Tramping Ground has baffled locals and intrigued visitors for generations. Despite being surrounded by lush forest, this barren circle remains void of any vegetation, earning it a reputation as a place of eerie silence and unsettling energy. Superstitions abound, with tales of those who dared to spend the night within the circle experiencing strange occurrences, from unexplained noises to inexplicable feelings of dread. Scientists have attempted to unravel the mystery, proposing theories ranging from soil composition to underground gases, yet the allure of the Devil's Tramping Ground persists, shrouded in myth and legend.

The Disappearance of the Sodder Children: In 1945, the Sodder family's home in West Virginia caught fire, leading to the mysterious disappearance of five of their children, despite extensive search efforts and investigations. Despite numerous theories and sightings over the years, the fate of the missing children remains unknown, fueling speculation about supernatural or paranormal involvement.

The Cottingley Fairies Hoax: In 1917, two young girls in England claimed to have photographed fairies in their garden, sparking a sensation and convincing even renowned author Sir Arthur Conan Doyle of their authenticity. The photographs were later revealed to be a hoax, created using cardboard cutouts, but the incident remains a fascinating example of how belief in the supernatural can influence perception and behavior.

The Enfield Poltergeist: The Enfield Poltergeist was a case of alleged poltergeist activity that occurred in a council house in Enfield, England, in the late 1970s. The haunting involved furniture moving by itself, objects levitating, and disembodied voices, captivating the attention of paranormal investigators and skeptics alike.

The Bell Witch Cave

The Bell Witch Cave in Tennessee holds a chilling legacy intertwined with tales of the supernatural. According to local lore, the cave is haunted by the vengeful spirit of Kate Batts, famously known as the Bell Witch, who terrorized the Bell family during the early 19th century. Over the years, visitors to the cave have reported experiencing eerie sensations, hearing unexplained noises echoing through its chambers, and even encountering ghostly apparitions. These unsettling encounters contribute to the cave's reputation as a hotspot for paranormal activity, drawing in curious visitors and paranormal enthusiasts alike to explore its mysterious depths and uncover the secrets hidden within its walls.

Notable Women in History

Ching Shih, the Pirate Queen

Ching Shih was one of the most successful pirates in history, commanding a fleet of over 1,500 ships and 80,000 pirates in the early 19th century. After her husband's death, she took control of his pirate confederation and implemented a strict code of conduct, with harsh punishments for disobedience, leading her to become one of the most feared and powerful figures on the high seas.

Khutulun, the Wrestling Princess: Khutulun, a Mongolian noblewoman and warrior princess, gained fame for her prowess in wrestling and horsemanship during the 13th century. Renowned for her strength and skill, she famously declared that she would only marry a man who could defeat her in wrestling, leading to numerous challengers and a legendary reputation on the battlefield.

Ida B. Wells, Anti-Lynching Crusader: Ida B. Wells was a pioneering African American journalist and civil rights activist who fought against racial injustice and lynching in the late 19th and early 20th centuries. She risked her life to investigate and expose the brutal realities of lynching in the United States, becoming one of the most prominent voices for racial equality and social justice.

Hedy Lamarr, Inventor and Actress: Hedy Lamarr, best known as a glamorous Hollywood actress of the 1930s and 1940s, was also an inventor who co-developed a frequency-hopping spread spectrum technology during World War II. Her invention, intended to secure radio communications for torpedoes, laid the groundwork for modern wireless communication technologies like Bluetooth and Wi-Fi, though her contributions were not widely recognized during her lifetime.

Lise Meitner's Nuclear Fission: Lise Meitner, an Austrian physicist, made significant contributions to the discovery of nuclear fission in the 20th century. Despite being excluded from the Nobel Prize awarded for this discovery, her groundbreaking work paved the way for the development of nuclear energy and atomic weapons, highlighting the often-overlooked contributions of women in scientific advancement.

Grace Hopper's Computer Programming: Grace Hopper, a pioneering computer scientist and United States Navy rear admiral, played a key role in the development of early computer programming languages, including COBOL. Her innovative work laid the foundation for modern software development and earned her the nickname "Amazing Grace" for her groundbreaking contributions to the field of computing. Her tireless advocacy for standardization and efficiency continues to influence programming practices today, cementing her legacy as one of the most influential figures in computer science history.

Sacagawea's Expedition

Sacagawea, a Shoshone woman, played a crucial role as an interpreter and guide during the Lewis and Clark Expedition in the early 19th century. Despite facing numerous challenges and dangers on the journey, Sacagawea's knowledge of the terrain and her diplomatic skills were instrumental in facilitating communication with Native American tribes and ensuring the success of the expedition.

Mary Anning's Fossil Discoveries: Mary Anning, a self-taught paleontologist in 19th-century England, made groundbreaking discoveries in the field of paleontology, including the first complete Ichthyosaur skeleton and the first Plesiosaur skeleton. Despite facing discrimination and financial hardship due to her gender and social status, Anning's contributions revolutionized our understanding of prehistoric life and laid the foundation for modern paleontological research.

Ada Lovelace's Computer Programming

Ada Lovelace, often regarded as the world's first computer programmer, wrote the first algorithm intended to be processed by a machine for Charles Babbage's Analytical Engine in the 19th century. Her visionary insights into the potential of computing laid the foundation for modern computer programming and earned her recognition as a pioneer of the digital age. Despite living in an era when women were largely excluded from scientific and technological fields, Lovelace's intellect and contributions to mathematics and computing were groundbreaking, challenging gender norms and inspiring future generations of women in STEM (Science, Technology, Engineering, and Mathematics) fields.

Gertrude Bell's Archaeological Expeditions: Gertrude Bell, a British archaeologist, explorer, and diplomat, played a key role in the excavation and preservation of archaeological sites in the Middle East in the early 20th century. Her extensive travels and scholarly contributions earned her the nickname "Queen of the Desert" and made her a respected authority on Middle Eastern archaeology and culture.

Annie Jump Cannon's Stellar Classification: Annie Jump Cannon, an American astronomer, developed the Harvard Classification Scheme for categorizing stars based on their spectral characteristics. Despite facing discrimination as a woman in the male-dominated field of astronomy, Cannon's groundbreaking work revolutionized our understanding of stellar evolution and laid the foundation for modern astrophysics.

Sojourner Truth's Abolitionist Activism: Sojourner Truth, an African American abolitionist and women's rights activist, delivered her famous "Ain't I a Woman?" speech at the Women's Rights Convention in Ohio in 1851. Her powerful advocacy for the rights of African Americans and women inspired generations of activists and cemented her legacy as a pioneering figure in the fight for equality and justice.

Anandi Gopal Joshi, India's First Female Doctor: Anandi Gopal Joshi was the first Indian woman to obtain a degree in Western medicine, earning her medical degree from the Women's Medical College of Pennsylvania in 1886. Despite facing numerous obstacles and societal expectations, Joshi's determination and perseverance paved the way for future generations of Indian women to pursue careers in medicine and education.

Rosalind Franklin's DNA Research: Rosalind Franklin, a British biophysicist, made crucial contributions to the understanding of DNA structure through her X-ray diffraction images, which provided key insights into the double helix structure of DNA. Despite her groundbreaking work, Franklin's contributions were often overshadowed by her male colleagues, highlighting the challenges faced by women in the male-dominated field of science. Franklin's legacy as a trailblazing scientist continues to be celebrated today, inspiring future generations of women in STEM fields and highlighting the importance of acknowledging the often-overlooked contributions of female scientists in history.

Hatshepsut's Reign as Pharaoh

Hatshepsut, one of ancient Egypt's most successful female pharaohs, ruled as co-regent with her stepson Thutmose III in the 15th century BCE. Despite efforts to erase her legacy from history, Hatshepsut's reign was marked by prosperity, innovation, and monumental building projects, making her one of Egypt's most remarkable and influential rulers. She ascended to power after the death of her husband and stepbrother, Thutmose II, and initially acted as regent for her young stepson before assuming the title of pharaoh herself, a move unprecedented in Egyptian history that challenged traditional gender roles and norms. Hatshepsut's reign saw significant advancements in trade, exploration, and artistic achievements, with her mortuary temple at Deir el-Bahari being one of the most impressive architectural marvels of ancient Egypt, showcasing her enduring legacy as a visionary leader.

Madam C.J. Walker's Entrepreneurial Success: Madam C.J. Walker, born Sarah Breedlove, was an African American entrepreneur and philanthropist who became one of the wealthiest self-made women in America in the early 20th century. Despite facing racial and gender discrimination, Walker built a successful beauty empire centered around hair care products for African American women and used her wealth to support charitable causes and social activism.

Noor Inayat Khan, WWII Spy: Noor Inayat Khan was a British secret agent of Indian descent who served as a wireless operator for the Special Operations Executive (SOE) during World War II. Despite facing grave danger as a spy behind enemy lines in Nazi-occupied France, Khan displayed remarkable courage and resilience, becoming the first female radio operator to be infiltrated into occupied territory and ultimately sacrificing her life for the Allied cause.

Nellie Bly's Record-breaking Trip: Nellie Bly, a pioneering investigative journalist in the late 19th century, gained international fame for her record-breaking trip around the world in 72 days. Inspired by Jules Verne's novel "Around the World in Eighty Days," Bly set out to beat the fictional record, embarking on a whirlwind journey that captivated the public imagination and solidified her reputation as a fearless and adventurous reporter.

Nellie Bly's Record-breaking Trip: Nellie Bly, a pioneering investigative journalist in the late 19th century, gained international fame for her record-breaking trip around the world in 72 days. Inspired by Jules Verne's novel "Around the World in Eighty Days," Bly set out to beat the fictional record, embarking on a whirlwind journey that captivated the public imagination and solidified her reputation as a fearless and adventurous reporter.

Harriet Tubman's Underground Railroad

Harriet Tubman, an African American abolitionist, and political activist became known as the "Moses of her people" for her role in leading hundreds of enslaved individuals to freedom through the Underground Railroad. Despite facing significant risks and dangers, Tubman's bravery and determination made her a legendary figure in the fight against slavery and injustice. Harriet Tubman's remarkable efforts didn't end with her involvement in the Underground Railroad; during the American Civil War, she served as a Union spy and scout, providing invaluable intelligence to the Union Army. After the war, Tubman continued her activism, advocating for women's suffrage and the rights of African Americans, demonstrating her lifelong commitment to social justice and equality.

Sappho, the Poetess of Lesbos: Sappho, an ancient Greek poet from the island of Lesbos, was renowned for her lyrical poetry and contributions to the genre of love poetry. Despite living in a patriarchal society, Sappho's work celebrated female desire and same-sex relationships, making her a pioneering figure in LGBTQ+ history and literature.

Legends of Exploration and Adventure

The Lost City of Z: The Lost City of Z, also known as El Dorado, is a legendary city said to be in the depths of the Amazon rainforest, filled with unimaginable riches. Despite numerous expeditions in search of this mythical city, no concrete evidence of its existence has ever been found, fueling speculation and fascination among explorers and adventurers.

The Search for Atlantis: Atlantis is a mythical island civilization described by the ancient Greek philosopher Plato in his dialogues. Despite centuries of speculation and exploration, the location of Atlantis remains a mystery, with theories placing it everywhere from the Mediterranean to the Caribbean

The White City of Honduras: The White City of Honduras, also known as the City of the Monkey God, is a fabled ancient settlement rumored to be hidden within the dense jungles of Mosquitia. In 2015, archaeologists announced the discovery of ruins matching the descriptions of the legendary city, including elaborately carved stone sculptures and artifacts, shedding new light on this enigmatic tale of exploration.

The Fountain of Youth: The Fountain of Youth is a mythical spring believed to bestow eternal youth and vitality upon those who drink from its waters. Explorers like Juan Ponce de León searched tirelessly for this legendary fountain in the New World, driven by the allure of immortality and the promise of endless adventure.

The Phantom Islands: Phantom islands are fictitious landmasses that appeared on maps during the Age of Exploration, often resulting from navigational errors, cartographic embellishments, or deliberate hoaxes. These elusive islands captured the imaginations of explorers and mapmakers, sparking quests to discover their hidden locations and uncover the mysteries of the uncharted seas.

The Tale of the Flying Dutchman

The legend of the Flying Dutchman has captivated sailors and storytellers for centuries, its origins lost to the mists of time. Tales of this phantom ship vary, but all share the common thread of a doomed captain condemned to sail the oceans eternally. According to some versions, the Flying Dutchman was cursed after its captain blasphemed during a storm, while others suggest it was lost in a wager with the devil. Regardless of its genesis, sightings of the ghostly vessel continue to be reported, sparking speculation and superstition among seafarers. Despite modern explanations attributing such sightings to optical illusions or atmospheric phenomena, the mystique of the Flying Dutchman endures, woven into the fabric of maritime folklore as a cautionary tale of hubris and eternal wandering.

The Curse of the Hope Diamond: The Hope Diamond, one of the world's most famous gemstones, is said to be cursed, bringing misfortune and tragedy to its owners. Legends tell of untimely deaths, financial ruin, and other calamities befalling those who possess or wear the cursed diamond, adding an aura of mystery and danger to its allure.

The Seven Cities of Gold: The Seven Cities of Gold, also known as the Cíbola, were legendary cities rumored to be filled with untold wealth and riches in the southwestern United States. Spanish conquistadors embarked on expeditions in search of these mythical cities, driven by greed and the desire for conquest, but found only harsh landscapes and indigenous civilizations.

The Hollow Earth Theory: The Hollow Earth Theory posits that the Earth is not a solid sphere but instead contains vast caverns and subterranean worlds inhabited by advanced civilizations. While widely dismissed by modern science, this concept has inspired explorers and adventurers throughout history, including attempts to locate hidden entrances to the inner Earth.

The Legend of Shangri-La: Shangri-La is a mythical Himalayan utopia described in James Hilton's novel "Lost Horizon," where inhabitants live in harmony and longevity. Inspired by Tibetan Buddhist beliefs and Himalayan landscapes, Shangri-La symbolizes an idyllic sanctuary untouched by the troubles of the outside world, captivating the imagination of adventurers and dreamers.

The Mysterious Disappearance of Amelia Earhart: Amelia Earhart, the pioneering aviator, disappeared without a trace during her attempt to circumnavigate the globe in 1937. Despite extensive search efforts and investigations, Earhart's fate remains one of the greatest mysteries in aviation history, fueling speculation and conspiracy theories about her disappearance.

The Legend of the Kraken: The Kraken is a legendary sea monster believed to dwell off the coasts of Norway and Greenland, capable of capsizing ships and dragging sailors to their watery graves. Described as a giant cephalopod resembling a colossal squid or octopus, the Kraken has inspired myths, legends, and maritime tales of terror for centuries.

The Legend of the Minotaur and the Labyrinth

In Greek mythology, the Minotaur is a monstrous creature with the body of a man and the head of a bull, imprisoned within the labyrinth of King Minos of Crete. Theseus, a legendary hero, ventured into the labyrinth to slay the Minotaur and free the people of Athens, symbolizing the triumph of courage and ingenuity over adversity.

The Roanoke Colony Mystery: The Roanoke Colony, established in present-day North Carolina in the late 16th century, mysteriously disappeared without a trace. The word "CROATOAN" carved into a tree and the letters "CRO" etched into a post were the only clues left behind, sparking centuries of speculation and theories about the fate of the lost colonists.

The Treasure of Oak Island: The Treasure of Oak Island has captured the fascination of treasure hunters and historians alike for centuries, shrouded in mystery and intrigue. Located off the coast of Nova Scotia, Canada, Oak Island's enigmatic past is steeped in legends of buried pirate treasure and possible connections to the Knights Templar. The allure of the island lies in its rumored booby traps, intricate underground tunnels, and cryptic symbols carved into stone, hinting at untold riches waiting to be uncovered.

The Quest for the Northwest Passage: The Northwest Passage is a fabled sea route through the Arctic connecting the Atlantic and Pacific Oceans. Explorers like John Franklin and Roald Amundsen braved the treacherous Arctic waters in search of this elusive passage, driven by the promise of a shortcut to the riches of the Far East.

The Legend of El Dorado: El Dorado is a mythical golden city believed to exist somewhere in the unexplored jungles of South America. Conquistadors like Francisco de Orellana and Gonzalo Pizarro embarked on perilous expeditions in search of this fabled city of gold, driven by the allure of wealth and glory.

The Mothman Legend: The Mothman is a cryptid creature reportedly sighted in the Point Pleasant area of West Virginia in the 1960s. Described as a winged humanoid with glowing red eyes, the Mothman is associated with premonitions of disaster and tragedy, leading to speculation about its origins and significance in local folklore. Despite numerous eyewitness accounts and the intense media coverage surrounding the sightings, the true nature of the Mothman remains a subject of debate, with theories ranging from a supernatural entity to a misidentified bird or owl species.

The Legend of King Arthur and the Holy Grail

The legend of King Arthur and the Holy Grail is a timeless narrative steeped in mystery and chivalry. At its heart lies the quest for the Holy Grail, a sacred relic believed to possess divine powers. According to lore, the Grail was the cup used by Jesus Christ during the Last Supper, imbued with mystical significance and the promise of spiritual enlightenment. This quest for the Holy Grail became a central theme in Arthurian legend, symbolizing the pursuit of virtue, righteousness, and the eternal quest for truth. As knights like Sir Galahad, Sir Percival, and Sir Lancelot venture forth in search of the Grail, they confront not only external adversaries but also the inner demons that test their mettle and challenge their resolve, serving as allegorical figures in the timeless quest for self-discovery and moral redemption. Through their trials and tribulations, the quest for the Holy Grail becomes a metaphor for the human condition, reminding us that true fulfillment lies not in material wealth or earthly power, but in the pursuit of virtue, righteousness, and the eternal quest for spiritual transcendence.

Historical Figures You've Never Heard Of

Khutulun: Khutulun, a Mongolian princess from the 13th century, was a formidable wrestler who demanded potential suitors to defeat her in wrestling for marriage. She reportedly remained undefeated and amassed a significant number of horses from her victories, making her one of the most remarkable female athletes in history.

Ibn Battuta: Ibn Battuta, a Moroccan explorer from the 14th century, embarked on a remarkable journey covering over 75,000 miles across Africa, Asia, and Europe. His travels lasted for nearly three decades, during which he visited numerous countries, documented his experiences in a detailed travelog called "Rihla," and served as a diplomat and judge in various Islamic courts.

Ynes Mexia: Ynes Mexia, a Mexican American botanist from the early 20th century, began her botanical career at the age of 55 and went on to become one of the most prolific plant collectors of her time. Over a span of 13 years, she collected over 150,000 plant specimens, many of which were new to science, and made significant contributions to botanical knowledge.

Humphry Davy: Humphry Davy, an English chemist from the late 18th and early 19th centuries, invented the Davy lamp, a safety lamp for miners that significantly reduced the risk of explosions in coal mines. His contributions to science also include discovering several chemical elements and pioneering the field of electrolysis.

Mansa Musa: Mansa Musa, a 14th-century emperor of the Mali Empire in West Africa, is often considered one of the wealthiest individuals in history. His pilgrimage to Mecca in 1324-1325, accompanied by a vast retinue and carrying immense amounts of gold, not only showcased the wealth of the Mali Empire but also inadvertently caused economic disruption in the regions he passed through due to his extravagant spending.

Q in Shi Huangdi

Qin Shi Huangdi, the first emperor of China from the Qin dynasty, is known for unifying China and constructing the Great Wall. However, he also ordered the burning of numerous books and the burial of scholars alive to suppress dissenting ideologies, earning him a reputation for tyranny and brutality.

Mary Anning: Mary Anning, an English fossil collector from the early 19th century, made significant contributions to paleontology by discovering numerous prehistoric fossils along the Jurassic Coast in England. Despite facing gender and class barriers, she unearthed several important specimens, including the first complete Ichthyosaur and Plesiosaur skeletons.

Giovanni Battista Belzoni: Giovanni Battista Belzoni, an Italian explorer and archaeologist from the late 18th and early 19th centuries, gained fame for his pioneering excavations of ancient Egyptian tombs and temples. He was known for his colossal size and strength, which he used to move massive artifacts and monuments, earning him the nickname "The Great Belzoni."

Aphra Behn: Aphra Behn, an English playwright and novelist from the 17th century, was one of the first professional female writers in English literature. Her works often explored themes of gender, power, and sexuality, challenging societal norms, and paving the way for future generations of women writers.

Sarah Baartman: Sarah Baartman, also known as the "Hottentot Venus," was a South African woman who was exhibited as a curiosity in Europe during the early 19th century due to her physical features, particularly her large buttocks. Her exploitation and objectification highlight the darker aspects of colonialism and racism in the 19th century.

Richard Francis Burton: Sir Richard Francis Burton, a British explorer and polymath from the 19th century, is renowned for his adventurous travels to exotic and often dangerous regions, including his journey to Mecca disguised as a Muslim pilgrim and his exploration of the source of the Nile River. He was also an accomplished linguist, translator, and author, publishing numerous books on his travels and studies.

Ibn al-Haytham: Ibn al-Haytham, an Arab mathematician, astronomer, and physicist from the 10th and 11th centuries, made significant contributions to the fields of optics and visual perception. His work on the nature of light and the formation of images laid the foundation for the modern science of optics and influenced European scientists later such as Roger Bacon and Johannes Kepler.

Nikola Tesla

Nikola Tesla, a Serbian American inventor and electrical engineer from the late 19th and early 20th centuries, made groundbreaking contributions to the development of alternating current (AC) electrical systems. Despite his significant achievements, including inventing the Tesla coil and pioneering wireless communication, he faced financial difficulties and died in relative obscurity.

Tlacaelel: Tlacaelel was a powerful advisor to several Aztec emperors in pre-Columbian Mexico and played a key role in shaping Aztec religious and political ideology. He implemented significant reforms, including the establishment of human sacrifice as a central tenet of Aztec religion and the promotion of militaristic expansionism.

Bass Reeves

Bass Reeves, an African American lawman from the late 19th and early 20th centuries, served as one of the first black deputy U.S. marshals west of the Mississippi River. Known for his exceptional marksmanship, tracking skills, and integrity, he captured over 3,000 criminals during his career and became a legendary figure in the American Old West.

Juana Inés de la Cruz: Sor Juana Inés de la Cruz, a Mexican nun and poet from the 17th century, was one of the most prominent literary figures of the Spanish Golden Age. Despite facing criticism and condemnation for her outspokenness and intellectual pursuits, she produced a vast body of poetry, essays, and plays that continue to be celebrated for their wit, intelligence, and feminist themes.

Grigori Rasputin

Grigori Rasputin, a Russian mystic, and advisor to the Romanov family in the early 20th century, gained considerable influence over Tsar Nicholas II and Tsarina Alexandra due to his purported healing abilities and mystical reputation. His controversial influence on Russian politics and his mysterious death by assassination have made him a figure of intrigue and speculation. Despite being poisoned, shot multiple times, and ultimately drowned in the Neva River, Rasputin's death remains shrouded in mystery, with various theories suggesting different perpetrators and motives behind the assassination.

Mary Seacole: Mary Seacole, a Jamaican-British nurse and businesswoman from the 19th century, played a significant role in providing medical care to wounded soldiers during the Crimean War. Despite facing racial prejudice and exclusion from Florence Nightingale's nursing corps, she established her own hospital and earned recognition for her compassion and dedication to nursing

Unsung Heroes of History

Rosie the Riveter: Although Rosie the Riveter is an iconic symbol of female empowerment during World War II, the real-life women who inspired the character remain relatively unknown. These women took on industrial jobs traditionally held by men, contributing significantly to the war effort by building planes, ships, and munitions. Their resilience and determination challenged gender stereotypes and paved the way for greater opportunities for women in the workforce.

Sydney Poitier: Sydney Poitier, a Bahamian-American actor, broke barriers in Hollywood during the mid-20th century, becoming the first Black actor to win an Academy Award for Best Actor. Despite facing discrimination and racial prejudice, Poitier achieved critical and commercial success with roles that challenged stereotypes and portrayed Black characters with dignity and complexity. His trailblazing career paved the way for greater representation and diversity in the film industry.

Elizebeth Friedman: Elizebeth Friedman was a pioneering codebreaker and cryptanalyst who played a vital role in cracking enemy codes during World War II. Working alongside her husband, William Friedman, she deciphered messages sent by Nazi spies and criminal organizations, contributing to Allied victories and national security. Friedman's groundbreaking work in cryptanalysis laid the groundwork for modern code breaking techniques and intelligence operations.

Ida B. Wells: Ida B. Wells was an African American investigative journalist, educator, and early leader in the civil rights movement. She fearlessly exposed the brutal realities of lynching in the Southern United States through her groundbreaking investigative journalism and advocacy. Wells' tireless efforts to combat racial injustice and promote civil rights paved the way for future activists and social reformers.

Gustav Whitehead

Gustav Whitehead, a German immigrant to the United States, conducted pioneering experiments in aviation in the late 19th and early 20th centuries. Some historians argue that Whitehead successfully flew a powered aircraft in 1901, two years before the Wright brothers' historic flight at Kitty Hawk. Whitehead's aircraft, the "Condor No. 21," purportedly achieved powered flight for about half a mile at a height of around 50 feet, as reported by eyewitnesses at the time. Despite controversy and skepticism surrounding his achievements, Whitehead's contributions to early aviation remain a subject of debate and fascination, with ongoing efforts to reassess and validate his place in aviation history.

Lise Meitner: Lise Meitner, an Austrian physicist, played a crucial role in the discovery of nuclear fission alongside Otto Hahn and Fritz Strassmann. Despite her significant contributions to the breakthrough, Meitner's male colleagues received the Nobel Prize in Chemistry for the discovery in 1944, while she was overlooked. Meitner's work laid the foundation for nuclear physics and highlighted the importance of recognizing women's contributions in science.

Simone Segouin: Simone Segouin, also known by her wartime alias Nicole Minet, was a French resistance fighter during World War II. At just 18 years old, she joined the resistance and participated in acts of sabotage against German forces, including derailing trains and ambushing enemy patrols. Segouin's bravery and unwavering commitment to the liberation of France earned her numerous decorations and commendations.

Annie Jump Cannon: Annie Jump Cannon was an American astronomer who developed the Harvard Classification Scheme, a system for categorizing and classifying stars based on their spectral characteristics. Despite facing hearing impairment, Cannon made significant contributions to the field of astronomy, cataloging hundreds of thousands of stars and paving the way for our modern understanding of stellar evolution. Her work laid the foundation for subsequent generations of astronomers.

Fred Korematsu: Fred Korematsu's fight against injustice resonates as strongly today as it did during World War II. Born in California in 1919, Korematsu challenged the constitutionality of Executive Order 9066, which authorized the internment of Japanese Americans during the war. Despite facing imprisonment and discrimination, he refused to accept the government's actions as lawful and took his case all the way to the Supreme Court. Although the Court ruled against him in Korematsu v. United States, Korematsu's legacy as a symbol of resistance to government overreach continues to inspire generations of civil rights activists.

Richard Proenneke

Richard Proenneke was an American outdoorsman who lived alone in the Alaskan wilderness for over 30 years, documenting his experiences through journals and films. In 1968, at the age of 51, he began constructing a cabin by hand near Twin Lakes, meticulously crafting every detail with basic hand tools and natural materials found in the wilderness. Proenneke's self-sufficient lifestyle included hunting, fishing, and cultivating his own food, showcasing his profound connection to the land and his ability to thrive in harmony with nature. Proenneke's simple yet extraordinary life in the wilderness continues to inspire generations of nature enthusiasts and homesteaders, serving as a testament to the human spirit's resilience and adaptability in the face of adversity.

Gertrude Bell: Gertrude Bell was a British archaeologist, explorer, and diplomat who played a significant role in shaping British policy in the Middle East during the early 20th century. Often referred to as the "female Lawrence of Arabia," Bell traveled extensively throughout the region, mapping uncharted territories, and establishing cultural connections with local tribes and leaders. Her insights and expertise influenced the creation of modern-day Iraq and Jordan, earning her the nickname "Queen of the Desert."

Vera Rubin: Vera Rubin was an American astronomer whose pioneering work provided compelling evidence for the existence of dark matter in the universe. Despite facing barriers as a woman in the male-dominated field of astronomy, Rubin's meticulous observations of the rotational speeds of galaxies revolutionized our understanding of cosmology. Her groundbreaking research laid the foundation for further exploration into the mysteries of the universe.

Katherine Johnson: Katherine Johnson was an African American mathematician whose calculations were critical to the success of NASA's early space missions, including John Glenn's historic orbit around the Earth. Despite facing racial and gender discrimination, Johnson's precise calculations of orbital mechanics were essential for the accuracy and safety of spaceflight. Her pioneering work at NASA helped pave the way for future generations of women and minorities in STEM fields.

Pauli Murray: Pauli Murray was a pioneering civil rights activist, lawyer, and Episcopal priest who fought tirelessly for gender and racial equality. As a co-founder of the National Organization for Women (NOW) and a legal strategist in the fight against segregation, Murray played a pivotal role in advancing civil rights and women's rights in the United States. Despite facing discrimination as an African American woman, Murray's advocacy and legal scholarship had a profound and lasting impact on American society.

Rosalind Franklin

Rosalind Franklin was a British chemist and X-ray crystallographer whose work was instrumental in elucidating the structure of DNA. Despite being overshadowed by her male colleagues, Franklin's X-ray diffraction images provided critical evidence for the double helix structure of DNA, a discovery that revolutionized our understanding of genetics. Her contributions to the field of molecular biology laid the groundwork for future breakthroughs in genetics and medicine.

.

Bayard Rustin: Bayard Rustin was a key architect of the civil rights movement in the United States, yet his contributions have often been overshadowed by other leaders. As a close advisor to Martin Luther King Jr., Rustin organized the historic March on Washington for Jobs and Freedom in 1963. He was a staunch advocate for nonviolent protest and played a vital role in shaping the strategies and tactics of the civil rights movement.

Charles Drew: Charles Drew was an African American physician, surgeon, and medical researcher who made pioneering contributions to the field of blood transfusion. He developed innovative techniques for the preservation and storage of blood plasma, revolutionizing transfusion medicine and saving countless lives. Despite facing racial discrimination, Drew's groundbreaking work laid the groundwork for the modern blood banking system.

Enver Hoxha's Bunker Obsession: Enver Hoxha, the communist leader of Albania, harbored intense paranoia about foreign invasion, leading him to construct an extensive network of bunkers across the country. These bunkers, numbering over 173,000, were built to withstand various forms of attack, ranging from conventional warfare to nuclear strikes, and became a pervasive feature of Albania's landscape during Hoxha's rule.

Sybil Ludington: Sybil Ludington, often dubbed the "female Paul Revere," bravely rode through the night to alert American colonial militias of an impending British attack during the Revolutionary War. Despite being only 16 years old at the time, her courageous act helped rally troops and thwart the British advance, yet her name remains relatively unknown compared to Revere's.

Jackie Mitchell: In 1931, Jackie Mitchell, a 17-year-old female pitcher, made headlines by striking out two of baseball's greatest players, Babe Ruth, and Lou Gehrig, during an exhibition game between the Chattanooga Lookouts and the New York Yankees. Mitchell's feat challenged gender stereotypes and showcased the talent of women in baseball, yet her achievements were largely overshadowed, and women were subsequently banned from playing professional baseball.

Influential Political Leaders

Winston Churchill's Love for Champagne: Churchill's love for champagne was not merely a casual indulgence but a deeply ingrained part of his persona. Despite the challenges and pressures of leading a nation through wartime, Churchill maintained a steadfast devotion to champagne, viewing it as a symbol of resilience and optimism in the face of adversity. His fondness for sparkling wine extended beyond personal enjoyment to diplomatic and political spheres, where he often used champagne to foster camaraderie and diplomacy with foreign leaders. Churchill's famous quote, "Remember, gentlemen, it's not just France we are fighting for, it's Champagne!" epitomizes his belief in the symbolic importance of the drink. His affinity for champagne not only added color to his public image but also underscored his appreciation for life's pleasures amidst the tumult of history.

Josip Broz Tito's Pet Alligator: Josip Broz Tito, the leader of Yugoslavia, had a peculiar fascination with exotic animals. Among his menagerie was a pet alligator named Mujo, which he received as a gift from Fidel Castro during a state visit. Mujo resided in a specially constructed pool within Tito's residence, where he became somewhat of a novelty among visiting dignitaries.

Kim Jong-il's Love for Basketball: Despite North Korea's isolation from much of the world, its leader Kim Jong-il developed a keen interest in basketball, particularly in the NBA. He reportedly had a personal collection of thousands of basketball videos and even authored a book on the sport. Despite his diminutive stature, Kim Jong-il fancied himself a basketball aficionado and occasionally engaged in exhibition matches with visiting dignitaries.

Idi Amin's Self-Proclaimed Titles: Idi Amin, the notorious dictator of Uganda, was known for his flamboyant and grandiose self-aggrandizement. His official title, "His Excellency, President for Life, Field Marshal Al Hadji Doctor Idi Amin Dada, VC, DSO, MC, Lord of All the Beasts of the Earth and Fishes of the Seas and Conqueror of the British Empire in Africa in General and Uganda in Particular," exemplified his megalomaniacal tendencies and delusions of grandeur.

Saparmurat Niyazov's Eccentric Dictatorship

Saparmurat Niyazov, the autocratic leader of Turkmenistan, ruled with an iron fist and eccentric flair. He renamed months and days of the week after himself and his family members, erected golden statues in his likeness that rotated to face the sun, and even authored a spiritual guidebook that became mandatory reading for all citizens. Niyazov's cult of personality reached absurd heights, cementing his status as one of the most bizarre dictators in history.

Muammar Gaddafi's Female Bodyguards: Muammar Gaddafi, the longtime ruler of Libya, surrounded himself with an elite cadre of female bodyguards known as the Amazonian Guard. Handpicked for their beauty, intelligence, and martial prowess, these bodyguards were sked with protecting Gaddafi at all costs and became a symbol of his eccentric and often unpredictable leadership style.

Robert Mugabe's Lavish Birthday Celebrations

Robert Mugabe, the former president of Zimbabwe, was known for his extravagant birthday celebrations, which served as a stark contrast to the economic hardships faced by most Zimbabweans. These lavish events, often held at luxurious resorts and attended by loyalists and sycophants, highlighted Mugabe's disconnect from the reality of his country's dire socio-economic situation. Despite widespread poverty and unemployment, Mugabe spared no expense on his birthday festivities, featuring lavish banquets, live performances, and extravagant gifts, further fueling criticism of his regime's corruption and mismanagement. Mugabe's opulent celebrations became emblematic of his authoritarian rule and his regime's disregard for the suffering of the Zimbabwean people, contributing to his eventual downfall amid widespread protests and international condemnation.

Augusto Pinochet's Helicopter Flight over the Andes: Augusto Pinochet, the military dictator of Chile, narrowly escaped an assassination attempt in 1986 when his helicopter was attacked by guerrillas while flying over the Andes Mountains. The daring attack, carried out by members of the Manuel Rodríguez Patriotic Front, highlighted the intense political turmoil and violence that characterized Pinochet's regime.

Mobutu Sese Seko's Cult of Personality: Mobutu Sese Seko, the dictator of Zaire (now the Democratic Republic of the Congo), cultivated a cult of personality around himself, presenting himself as the father and savior of the nation. His image was ubiquitous in Zaire, adorning billboards, posters, and currency, while dissent and opposition were ruthlessly suppressed. Mobutu's extravagant lifestyle and despotic rule fueled widespread corruption and economic decline, ultimately leading to his ousting from power.

François Duvalier's Use of Voodoo: François Duvalier, known as "Papa Doc," exploited Haiti's deeply ingrained voodoo traditions to consolidate his power and instill fear among the populace. Duvalier presented himself as a mythical figure with supernatural powers, invoking voodoo rituals and symbols to maintain control over his subjects and quash dissent. The Tonton Macoute, Duvalier's feared paramilitary force, often employed voodoo symbolism and practices to intimidate and terrorize the Haitian people.

Slobodan Milošević's Unorthodox Defense Tactics: During his trial for war crimes at the International Criminal Tribunal for the former Yugoslavia, Slobodan Milošević opted to represent himself in court, employing unorthodox tactics to delay proceedings and assert his political agenda. Milošević used the trial as a platform to promote Serbian nationalism and challenge the legitimacy of the tribunal, engaging in lengthy cross-examinations and delivering impassioned speeches that sought to delegitimize the court's authority.

Park Chung-hee's Famed Tousled Hair

Park Chung-hee, the authoritarian leader of South Korea, was known for his distinctive tousled hairstyle, which became emblematic of his authoritarian rule. Park's unruly hairdo was often cited as a symbol of his strong-willed and uncompromising demeanor, reflecting his reputation as a strongman ruler who brooked no opposition.

Juan Perón's Love for Eva Perón: Juan Perón, the populist leader of Argentina, idolized his wife, Eva Perón, and elevated her to near-sainthood status during her lifetime and after her death. Eva, affectionately known as "Evita," wielded considerable influence over Argentine politics and society, championing social welfare programs and women's rights initiatives. Perón's unwavering devotion to Eva and her enduring legacy as a champion of the poor and marginalized continue to shape Argentine politics to this day.

Manuel Noriega's Ties to Drug Trafficking: Manuel Noriega, the military dictator of Panama, became deeply involved in drug trafficking and money laundering schemes, forging alliances with Colombian drug cartels and accepting bribes in exchange for protection. Noriega's illicit activities attracted the attention of U.S. authorities, leading to his indictment on drug trafficking charges and eventual capture during the 1989 U.S. invasion of Panama.

Mao Zedong's Swim in the Yangtze River

Mao Zedong's swim in the Yangtze River at the age of 73 was not only a symbolic act but also a highly orchestrated event aimed at bolstering his image as a strong and capable leader. The swim was a calculated propaganda move, carefully planned, and executed by Mao's advisors and the state media. It served to reinforce the narrative of Mao as a charismatic and invincible leader, capable of defying age and adversity. However, some historians argue that the swim was staged, with reports suggesting that Mao swam only a short distance before being assisted by aides due to his declining health. Despite the controversy surrounding the event, Mao's swim remains a notable episode in the history of Chinese propaganda and political theater.

Fulgencio Batista's Lavish Lifestyle: Fulgencio Batista, the dictator of Cuba, led a life of luxury and excess, frequenting casinos, nightclubs, and extravagant parties while amassing immense wealth through corruption and exploitation. Batista's opulent lifestyle stood in stark contrast to the poverty and oppression experienced by most Cubans under his rule, fueling widespread discontent and revolutionary sentiment that ultimately culminated in the Cuban Revolution led by Fidel Castro.

Napoleon Bonaparte's Fear of Cats: Napoleon Bonaparte's fear of cats is a peculiar aspect of his personality that sheds light on the complex psyche of one of history's most formidable figures. Despite his reputation for fearlessness on the battlefield, Napoleon's aversion to cats reveals a vulnerability and superstition that contrast with his image as a rational and calculating leader. Some historians have suggested that Napoleon's fear may have stemmed from childhood experiences or cultural beliefs about cats as symbols of bad luck or malevolence. Whatever the cause, Napoleon's apprehension towards felines offers a fascinating glimpse into the human side of a man who wielded immense power and influence on the world stage.

Benito Mussolini's Affinity for Futurism: Benito Mussolini, the fascist dictator of Italy, was a staunch supporter of the Futurist movement, which glorified modernity, speed, and technological advancement. Mussolini commissioned numerous architectural projects and propaganda campaigns that embraced Futurist aesthetics, symbolizing his vision of Italy as a modern and dynamic nation at the forefront of progress. Mussolini's embrace of the Futurist movement extended beyond architecture to include literature, art, and even urban planning, where he sought to reshape Italian cities according to Futurist principles. However, the alliance between Mussolini's regime and the Futurists eventually soured due to ideological differences and the movement's waning influence, leading to its decline in the late 1930s.

Famous Inventors and Their Inventions

Thomas Edison's Spirit Phone: Edison, renowned for his inventions like the light bulb and phonograph, attempted to create a device to communicate with the dead. Known as the "spirit phone" or "ethereal phone," Edison believed that his invention could capture messages from the afterlife but ultimately abandoned the project due to lack of success.

Nikola Tesla's Earthquake Machine: Tesla claimed to have developed a mechanical oscillator capable of generating powerful vibrations that could potentially cause earthquakes. While Tesla conducted experiments to test his theory, including one at his laboratory in New York, there is no evidence to support the effectiveness of his alleged earthquake machine.

Mary Anderson: Best known for inventing the windshield wiper in 1903 after observing a streetcar driver struggling to see through a sleet-covered windshield. Anderson's manually operated device, initially dismissed by auto manufacturers, eventually became standard equipment on all automobiles, enhancing driver safety and comfort.

Benjamin Franklin's Musical Glasses: In addition to his renowned experiments with electricity, Benjamin Franklin invented a musical instrument called the glass armonica. Consisting of glass bowls of varying sizes mounted on a spindle, the armonica produced ethereal, haunting tones when played by rubbing the rims with wet fingers.

Alexander Graham Bell's Tetrahedral Kites: While best known for inventing the telephone, Alexander Graham Bell also experimented with aviation and developed tetrahedral kites made of interconnected triangular frames. These innovative kites paved the way for advancements in aeronautics and influenced the design of early aircraft.

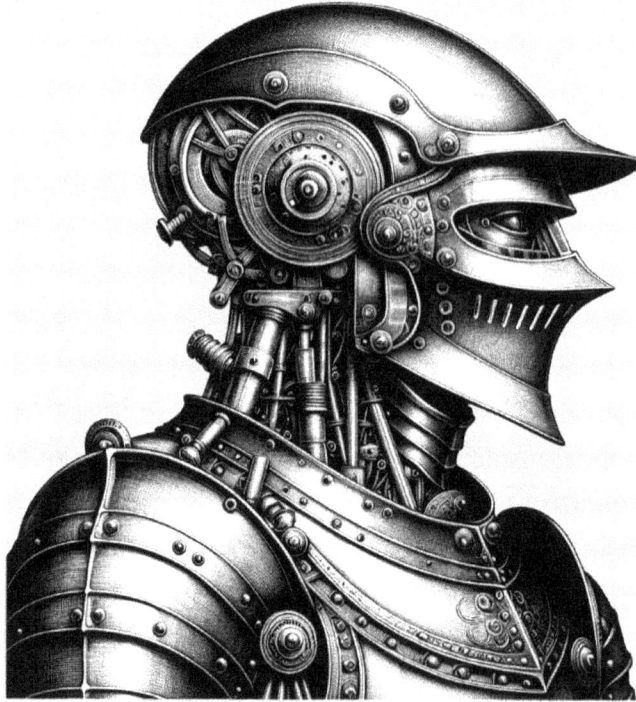

Leonardo da Vinci's Robot Knight

Leonardo da Vinci designed a humanoid robot knight in the late 15th century, complete with articulated joints and a programmable system of pulleys and cables. Although the robot was never built during his lifetime, da Vinci's detailed sketches and concepts laid the groundwork for future advancements in robotics. His design included mechanisms for the robot to sit, stand, move its head, and even lift its visor, showcasing his intricate understanding of anatomy and mechanical engineering. Despite the limitations of the technology available in his time, da Vinci's vision for a mechanical creation capable of mimicking human motion and interaction foreshadowed the development of modern robotics centuries later.

Henry Ford's Soybean Car: In 1941, Henry Ford unveiled a car made primarily from soybean-based plastic, derived from soybeans grown on his own farmland. Ford's "plastic car" was intended to be lightweight, durable, and environmentally friendly, but production was halted due to the outbreak of World War II and the focus on wartime manufacturing.

George Washington Carver's Peanut Recipes: While George Washington Carver is renowned for his research on peanuts and other crops, he also developed hundreds of peanut-based recipes, including peanut butter cookies and peanut soup. Carver's culinary innovations helped popularize peanuts as a versatile and nutritious ingredient in American cuisine.

Chester Greenwood: a teenager from Maine, invented earmuffs at the age of 15 in 1873 to protect his ears while ice skating. His simple but ingenious design, made from wire frames and fur, quickly gained popularity, and Greenwood went on to patent his invention, becoming one of the youngest inventors in history.

Elisha Otis' Elevator Safety Brake: Elisha Otis invented the safety elevator with a mechanical brake that engaged in the event of a cable failure, preventing the elevator from plummeting. Otis famously demonstrated the reliability of his invention at the 1854 New York World's Fair by riding an elevator and ordering the rope to be cut, showcasing its life-saving capabilities.

Wilhelm Conrad Roentgen's X-Ray Photography: Wilhelm Conrad Roentgen accidentally discovered X-rays while experimenting with cathode rays in his laboratory. His serendipitous discovery revolutionized medical diagnostics by allowing physicians to visualize internal structures of the body without invasive procedures, earning Roentgen the first Nobel Prize in Physics in 1901.

George de Mestral's Velcro Inspiration: Swiss engineer George de Mestral was inspired to invent Velcro after observing how burrs stuck to his dog's fur during a walk in the Swiss Alps. De Mestral replicated the burr's hook-and-loop mechanism using nylon and polyester, leading to the creation of Velcro as a versatile fastening material.

Archimedes' Heat Ray Myth: Legend has it that the ancient Greek mathematician Archimedes designed a "heat ray" weapon to defend the city of Syracuse from invading Roman ships. While the exact nature of Archimedes' invention remains uncertain, modern experiments suggest that a large array of mirrors could potentially focus sunlight to ignite wooden ships.

Guglielmo Marconi's Wireless Telegraphy: Guglielmo Marconi developed the first practical system of wireless telegraphy, transmitting radio signals across long distances without the need for wires. Marconi's pioneering work laid the foundation for modern radio communication and earned him the Nobel Prize in Physics in 1909.

Marie Curie's Mobile Radiography Units: Marie Curie, famous for her groundbreaking research on radioactivity, developed mobile radiography units, also known as "Little Curies," to provide X-ray services to field hospitals during World War I. These portable units revolutionized medical diagnostics on the battlefield, saving countless lives by enabling rapid detection of injuries and fractures.

John Boyd Dunlop's Pneumatic Bicycle Tire: John Boyd Dunlop invented the pneumatic bicycle tire in 1888, using an inflatable rubber tube encased in a fabric casing to provide a smoother and more comfortable ride. Dunlop's invention significantly improved cycling performance and comfort, leading to widespread adoption and shaping the future of transportation.

Robert Fulton's Nautilus Submarine

Robert Fulton's Nautilus submarine represents a remarkable intersection of innovation and naval history. Commissioned by Napoleon Bonaparte in 1800, the Nautilus was a pioneering attempt at creating a practical submarine. Despite its early success in underwater demonstrations, the Nautilus failed to garner widespread military adoption. However, Fulton's groundbreaking work laid the groundwork for subsequent advancements in submarine technology, influencing future designs and contributing to the eventual integration of submarines into naval warfare. The Nautilus stands as a testament to Fulton's ingenuity and vision, highlighting his significant contributions to both maritime engineering and military strategy during the early 19th century.

Madame C.J. Walker's Hair Care Products: Madame C.J. Walker, the first female self-made millionaire in America, revolutionized the hair care industry for African American women by developing a line of hair care products. Walker's innovative hair treatments and scalp ointments addressed common issues faced by women of color, empowering them to embrace their natural hair textures.

Steve Jobs' Apple Lisa Flop

Before the Macintosh, Apple introduced the Lisa computer, named after Steve Jobs' daughter, in 1983. Despite its advanced features, including a graphical user interface and mouse, the Lisa was a commercial failure due to its exorbitant price and limited software compatibility.

Albert Einstein's Refrigerator Patent: Albert Einstein's foray into refrigerator technology represents a lesser-known aspect of his multifaceted genius. Alongside physicist Leo Szilard, Einstein sought to address the safety concerns associated with conventional refrigeration methods by developing a safer alternative. Their refrigerator design utilized compressed gases, such as butane and propane, which posed fewer risks compared to the hazardous chemicals commonly used at the time. Despite their innovative approach, technical obstacles and the emergence of more efficient cooling technologies hindered the widespread adoption of the Einstein-Szilard refrigerator. Nonetheless, Einstein's involvement in this practical endeavor highlights his commitment to humanitarian causes and his willingness to apply scientific principles to real-world problems beyond the realm of theoretical physics.

Famous Literary Figures and Their Works

Lewis Carroll's Hidden Love Letters: Lewis Carroll, author of "Alice's Adventures in Wonderland," was known for his unconventional hobbies, including photography and writing. However, lesser known are his cryptic acrostic poems, believed to contain hidden messages expressing his love for Alice Liddell, the inspiration for Alice in Wonderland.

The Mysterious Manuscript of Marcel Proust: Marcel Proust, author of "In Search of Lost Time," is known for his sprawling, introspective novel exploring memory and time. However, a lesser-known fact is that Proust's original manuscript was famously lost and only rediscovered years later in a Parisian garage, sparking intrigue and speculation among literary scholars.

Agatha Christie's Disappearance: Agatha Christie, the queen of mystery fiction and creator of iconic detectives like Hercule Poirot and Miss Marple, experienced a real-life mystery of her own. In 1926, she disappeared for 11 days under mysterious circumstances, sparking a massive manhunt and countless theories about her whereabouts before reappearing with no memory of her disappearance.

H.P. Lovecraft's Fear of Cats: H.P. Lovecraft, the master of cosmic horror and creator of the Cthulhu Mythos, harbored an unusual fear: cats. Despite featuring feline-like creatures in his stories, Lovecraft was reportedly terrified of actual cats, believing them to be supernatural beings capable of perceiving otherworldly entities.

Virginia Woolf's Manuscript in the River: Virginia Woolf, renowned for her modernist novels like "Mrs. Dalloway" and "To the Lighthouse," had a tumultuous relationship with her writing. In a fit of despair, she once tossed the manuscript of her novel "The Waves" into the river Ouse, only to retrieve it later with the help of a local boatman.

Emily Dickinson's Secret Compartment

The reclusive poet Emily Dickinson, renowned for her introspective verses, had a penchant for privacy. However, upon her death, a hidden compartment was discovered in her room containing over 40 handwritten poems, shedding new light on her prolific output and personal struggles.

Mark Twain's Obsession with White Suits: Mark Twain, celebrated for his wit and satire in works like "The Adventures of Huckleberry Finn," had an eccentric fashion sense. He became so enamored with white suits in his later years that he often wore them exclusively, even going so far as to suggest that they represented purity and moral integrity.

Ernest Hemingway's Six-Toed Cats: Ernest Hemingway, the Nobel Prize-winning author known for his terse prose and adventurous lifestyle, had a peculiar fondness for six-toed cats. He adopted numerous polydactyl cats, descendants of a six-toed cat named Snow White, which still roam his former home in Key West, Florida, now a museum.

Charlotte Brontë's Imaginary World: Charlotte Brontë, author of "Jane Eyre," had a vivid imagination from a young age and, along with her siblings, created an elaborate imaginary world called Angria. This fictional universe served as the backdrop for their childhood stories and later influenced Charlotte's writing as she explored themes of passion and rebellion.

Oscar Wilde's Unpublished Work: Oscar Wilde, known for his wit and flamboyant lifestyle, wrote much more than his famous plays and essays. After his death, a treasure trove of unpublished manuscripts and fragments was discovered, including drafts of plays, poems, and letters, offering new insights into his creative process and private thoughts.

Edgar Allan Poe's Coded Messages: Edgar Allan Poe, master of macabre tales like "The Tell-Tale Heart" and "The Raven," was fascinated by cryptography. He often incorporated secret codes and ciphers into his writings, challenging readers to decipher hidden messages and unravel the mysteries within his stories.

Dante Alighieri's Unfinished Masterpiece: Dante Alighieri, author of the epic poem "The Divine Comedy," left behind an unfinished masterpiece at the time of his death. Titled "The Comedy," this ambitious work was intended to be a comprehensive encyclopedia of human knowledge, exploring theology, philosophy, and science in verse.

Mary Shelley's Heart Keepsake: Mary Shelley, author of "Frankenstein," had a unique memento of her deceased husband, Percy Bysshe Shelley. After his death, she carried his calcified heart with her everywhere she went, wrapped in the pages of his poetry, serving as a morbid yet poignant symbol of their enduring love.

Jorge Luis Borges' Imaginary Libraries

Jorge Luis Borges, the Argentine writer known for his innovative short stories and essays, often explored themes of infinity and labyrinthine structures in his work. He famously described imaginary libraries containing every possible book ever written, reflecting his fascination with the limitless possibilities of literature and knowledge.

Sylvia Plath's Telepathic Connection: Sylvia Plath, the acclaimed poet and author of "The Bell Jar," believed in the power of telepathy and claimed to have experienced psychic connections with her husband, Ted Hughes. She documented these experiences in her journals, blurring the lines between reality and imagination in her quest for deeper understanding.

Jack Kerouac's Scroll Manuscript: Jack Kerouac, leader of the Beat Generation and author of "On the Road," wrote his groundbreaking novel in a legendary burst of creativity fueled by coffee and Benzedrine. He famously typed the entire manuscript on a single continuous scroll of paper, eschewing traditional formatting and editing in favor of spontaneity and raw expression.

J.K. Rowling's Rejection Letters: Before achieving worldwide fame with the "Harry Potter" series, J.K. Rowling faced numerous rejections from publishers. However, one rejection letter stands out as particularly memorable: it advised her to get a day job because there was no money in children's books. Rowling's perseverance and belief in her storytelling ultimately led to one of the most successful literary franchises in history.

F Scott Fitzgerald's Obsession with Lists: F. Scott Fitzgerald, renowned for his novel "The Great Gatsby," had a peculiar habit of making lists throughout his life. These lists ranged from practical reminders and literary ideas to profound reflections on life and death, offering glimpses into the mind of the iconic Jazz Age author.

T.S. Eliot's Secret Identity: T.S. Eliot, the modernist poet behind works like "The Waste Land" and "The Love Song of J. Alfred Prufrock," had a secretive alter ego known as "Old Possum." Under this pseudonym, he wrote whimsical poems about cats, later compiled into the beloved children's book "Old Possum's Book of Practical Cats."

Revolutionary Scientific Discoveries

Vitamin C's Role in Scurvy Prevention: In the 18th century, British naval surgeon James Lind conducted one of the earliest controlled experiments, demonstrating that citrus fruits could prevent and treat scurvy among sailors. Despite the simplicity and effectiveness of his findings, it took several decades before the British Navy officially adopted citrus fruits to combat scurvy, highlighting the slow acceptance of scientific evidence in the medical community.

The Cosmic Microwave Background Radiation: In 1965, Arno Penzias and Robert Wilson discovered cosmic microwave background radiation, providing strong evidence for the Big Bang theory of the universe's origin. Their accidental discovery, made while investigating radio interference, earned them the Nobel Prize in Physics in 1978 and revolutionized our understanding of the universe's early history.

The Double Helix Structure of DNA: In 1953, James Watson and Francis Crick proposed the double helix structure of DNA, based on X-ray diffraction images captured by Rosalind Franklin and Maurice Wilkins. Despite controversy surrounding the use of Franklin's data without her consent, Watson, Crick, and Wilkins were awarded the Nobel Prize in Physiology or Medicine in 1962 for their groundbreaking discovery, which laid the foundation for modern molecular biology.

The Discovery of the Higgs Boson: In 2012, scientists at CERN's Large Hadron Collider announced the discovery of the Higgs boson, a subatomic particle predicted by the Standard Model of particle physics. The discovery confirmed the existence of the Higgs field, which gives particles mass, and provided crucial validation for the Standard Model, our current understanding of the fundamental particles and forces that make up the universe.

The Discovery of Penicillin's Antibacterial Properties

In 1928, Scottish bacteriologist Alexander Fleming accidentally discovered the antibacterial properties of penicillin when he observed mold inhibiting the growth of bacteria on a petri dish. Despite the potential of his discovery, it wasn't until the 1940s that penicillin was successfully mass-produced and widely used as the first antibiotic, revolutionizing medicine, and saving countless lives.

The Theory of Plate Tectonics: In the early 20th century, Alfred Wegener proposed the theory of continental drift, suggesting that Earth's continents were once joined together in a single supercontinent called Pangaea. Despite facing skepticism from the scientific community, Wegener's theory laid the groundwork for the modern theory of plate tectonics, revolutionizing our understanding of Earth's geological processes and the dynamics of its surface.

The Discovery of Neutron Stars: In 1967, astrophysicist Jocelyn Bell Burnell and her advisor Antony Hewish discovered the first pulsar, a rapidly rotating neutron star emitting regular pulses of radio waves. Burnell's discovery challenged existing theories of stellar evolution and neutron stars, earning her widespread recognition, and paving the way for new discoveries in astrophysics.

147

The Theory of Relativity's Prediction of Gravitational Lensing: In 1915, Albert Einstein's theory of general relativity predicted the phenomenon of gravitational lensing, in which the gravity of massive objects bends and distorts the paths of light rays, leading to the observation of multiple images of distant objects. Despite initial skepticism, gravitational lensing has since become a powerful tool for studying the distribution of matter in the universe and confirming the predictions of Einstein's theory.

The Discovery of the Endocannabinoid System: In the late 20th century, scientists discovered the endocannabinoid system, a complex network of receptors and neurotransmitters involved in regulating various physiological processes. Despite the long history of cannabis use, the endocannabinoid system was only identified in the 1980s and 1990s, leading to new insights into the effects of cannabinoids on the body and potential therapeutic applications for various medical conditions.

The Synthesis of Artificial Elements: In the 20th century, scientists successfully synthesized artificial elements beyond uranium, expanding the periodic table and challenging our understanding of atomic structure. Despite the complex and challenging nature of these experiments, researchers have continued to push the boundaries of synthetic chemistry, creating new elements with increasingly higher atomic numbers.

The Discovery of Gravitational Waves: In 2015, scientists announced the first direct detection of gravitational waves, ripples in spacetime caused by the collision of massive objects like black holes or neutron stars. Despite being predicted by Albert Einstein's theory of general relativity a century earlier, gravitational waves had eluded detection until the development of advanced gravitational wave detectors like LIGO and Virgo, opening a new window to observe the universe.

The Discovery of CRISPR-Cas9 Gene Editing

The discovery of the CRISPR-Cas9 gene editing system stands as a watershed moment in the field of molecular biology. In the early 21st century, researchers elucidated the mechanisms by which certain bacteria defend against viral infections using clustered regularly interspaced short palindromic repeats (CRISPR) and the Cas9 enzyme. This breakthrough paved the way for the development of a versatile gene editing tool that enables scientists to precisely target and modify specific sequences of DNA with unprecedented accuracy. Since its discovery, CRISPR-Cas9 has revolutionized biological research by offering a streamlined and cost-effective method for genome editing, with far-reaching implications for medical treatments, agricultural advancements, and biotechnological innovations. Its potential to address genetic disorders, engineer disease-resistant crops, and even combat infectious diseases has sparked immense excitement and anticipation within the scientific community and beyond, heralding a new era of genetic manipulation and discovery.

The Discovery of Quasars: In the 1960s, astronomers discovered quasars, incredibly bright and distant objects powered by supermassive black holes at the centers of galaxies. Despite their small size and immense distance from Earth, quasars emit vast amounts of energy, providing valuable insights into the early universe and the dynamics of galactic nuclei.

The Development of RNA Interference (RNAi) Technology: In the late 20th century, scientists discovered RNA interference (RNAi), a natural cellular process for regulating gene expression by silencing specific RNA molecules. Despite its initial discovery in plants and animals, RNAi has since become a powerful tool for studying gene function and has potential applications in medicine, agriculture, and biotechnology.

The Discovery of Dark Energy: In the late 20th century, astronomers observed that the expansion of the universe was accelerating, leading to the discovery of dark energy, a mysterious force driving the universe's accelerated expansion. Despite its enigmatic nature, dark energy is thought to make up the majority of the universe's energy density, challenging our understanding of fundamental physics and cosmology.

The Confirmation of Dark Matter: The confirmation of dark matter represents a pivotal moment in our exploration of the universe's mysteries. In the late 20th century, astrophysicists amassed compelling evidence for the existence of dark matter through observations of galaxy rotation curves, gravitational lensing, and the large-scale structure of the cosmos. Despite its pervasive influence, dark matter eludes direct detection and identification, remaining undetectable through electromagnetic radiation. This enigmatic substance comprises around 85% of the universe's total mass, exerting gravitational forces that shape the cosmic landscape on cosmic scales. Decades of research have deepened our understanding of dark matter's role in galactic dynamics and cosmic evolution, yet its true nature continues to elude scientists, fueling ongoing investigations and theoretical speculation into its properties and interactions.

The Discovery of Exoplanets

The discovery of exoplanets, planets orbiting stars beyond our solar system, marks a profound shift in our understanding of the cosmos. In the 1990s, astronomers, utilizing increasingly sophisticated observational techniques, detected the first confirmed exoplanets, challenging the long-held belief that our solar system was unique. Since then, the field of exoplanet research has exploded, with thousands of exoplanets identified to date, ranging from gas giants to rocky terrestrial worlds. This wealth of newfound celestial bodies has sparked a renaissance in astrophysics, driving efforts to characterize these distant worlds and assess their potential for harboring life. Indeed, the discovery of exoplanets has not only expanded our cosmic perspective but also ignited hope for the possibility of finding extraterrestrial life beyond Earth, fueling the imagination of scientists and the public alike.

The Development of Carbon Nanotubes: In the late 20th century, scientists discovered carbon nanotubes, cylindrical molecules made of carbon atoms with remarkable strength, flexibility, and electrical conductivity. Despite their simple structure, carbon nanotubes have a wide range of potential applications in electronics, materials science, and nanotechnology, revolutionizing various industries and technologies. In addition to their structural properties, carbon nanotubes exhibit unique thermal conductivity, making them promising candidates for applications in heat management and thermal interface materials, further expanding their potential impact across diverse fields such as aerospace, energy storage, and biomedical engineering.

The Discovery of the Archaea Domain: In the late 20th century, scientists discovered the Archaea domain, a distinct group of single-celled microorganisms with characteristics of both bacteria and eukaryotes. Despite their initial classification as bacteria, advances in molecular biology and DNA sequencing revealed that Archaea represents a separate domain of life, challenging our understanding of microbial diversity and evolution. The discovery of the Archaea domain revolutionized our understanding of microbial life and evolutionary biology. Their unique biology, including the presence of distinct RNA polymerases and cell membranes, distinguished them from both bacteria and eukaryotes, leading to their classification as a separate domain of life. This discovery not only expanded our knowledge of microbial diversity but also raised intriguing questions about the origins and evolution of cellular life on Earth, prompting scientists to reevaluate the tree of life and the relationships between different branches of organisms.

Remarkable Animal Kingdom Facts

Electric Eels' Shocking Abilities: Electric eels, found in South America, possess specialized electric organs that can discharge high-voltage electric shocks to stun prey or deter predators. These shocks are produced by thousands of specialized cells called electrocytes, arranged in series, which create a powerful electrical field around the eel's body.

The Immortal Jellyfish: Turritopsis dohrnii, known as the immortal jellyfish, has the unique ability to transform its mature adult cells back into immature cells, effectively reverting its aging process and allowing it to rejuvenate itself. When faced with environmental stress or physical damage, the jellyfish can undergo a process called trans differentiation, where it converts its cells into a younger state, giving it potentially indefinite longevity.

The Bizarre Axolotl: Axolotls, native to Mexico, are renowned for their remarkable regenerative abilities, capable of regrowing lost limbs, organs, and even parts of their brain throughout their lifespan. This regenerative prowess has made axolotls a valuable model organism for studying tissue repair and regeneration in biomedical research.

The Unusual Platypus: Platypuses, found in Australia, are one of the few mammals that lay eggs instead of giving birth to live young, a trait known as oviparity. Additionally, male platypuses possess venomous spurs on their hind legs, capable of delivering a painful sting that can incapacitate or deter potential threats.

The Resourceful Sea Cucumber: Sea cucumbers have a fascinating defense mechanism known as evisceration, where they expel their internal organs, such as their respiratory trees and digestive tract, as a means of deterring predators. Despite appearing gruesome, sea cucumbers can regenerate their lost organs within a matter of weeks, allowing them to recover from predation attempts and continue their lives relatively unharmed.

The Surprising Star-Nosed Mole

Star-nosed moles, found in North America, have a distinctive star-shaped appendage on their nose known as the Eimer's organ, which contains over 25,000 sensory receptors called Eimer's corpuscles. These highly sensitive touch receptors allow the mole to detect and identify prey underwater with astonishing speed and accuracy, enabling it to forage efficiently in its aquatic habitat. The star-shaped nose of the star-nosed mole is the most sensitive known touch organ of any mammal, allowing it to detect prey in less than a quarter of a second, making it one of the fastest hunters among mammals. This remarkable adaptation enables the star-nosed mole to thrive in its specialized niche as a semi-aquatic predator, demonstrating the fascinating diversity of evolutionary strategies in the animal kingdom.

The Incredible Mimic Octopus: The mimic octopus, native to the waters of Southeast Asia, possesses an extraordinary ability to mimic the appearance and behavior of other marine creatures, including venomous species such as lionfish and sea snakes. By changing color, shape, and movement, the mimic octopus can convincingly imitate its surroundings, allowing it to evade predators and ambush prey with remarkable precision.

Japanese Giant Hornets' Defensive Tactics: Japanese giant hornets, among the largest hornets in the world, employ a formidable defense strategy against threats to their colony. When threatened, they release a pheromone that summons reinforcements, allowing them to overwhelm intruders with a coordinated attack, capable of killing small animals and even humans.

The Astounding Lyrebird: Lyrebirds, found in Australia, are renowned for their remarkable ability to mimic a wide range of sounds, including other bird species, animals, and even human-made noises such as car alarms and chainsaws. Male lyrebirds use their impressive vocal mimicry skills during courtship displays to attract mates and establish their territory.

The Curious Hoatzin: Hoatzins, native to South America, have a unique digestive system that produces methane gas as a byproduct of fermentation, giving them their characteristic foul odor. Additionally, hoatzin chicks possess specialized claws on their wings, which they use to climb trees and branches shortly after hatching, a trait believed to be an evolutionary remnant from their dinosaur ancestors.

The Extraordinary Sea Slug: Some species of sea slugs, such as Elysia chlorotica, have a remarkable ability to incorporate chloroplasts from the algae they consume into their own cells, allowing them to perform photosynthesis and generate energy from sunlight. This unique symbiotic relationship with algae provides sea slugs with a supplementary source of nutrition and enables them to thrive in sunlit shallow waters.

The Mysterious Sea Pig: Sea pigs, deep-sea dwelling relatives of sea cucumbers, play a vital role in oceanic ecosystems by consuming detritus and marine snow that falls from the surface, effectively recycling nutrients and maintaining a clean seafloor. Despite their unassuming appearance, sea pigs are an essential component of deep-sea food webs, providing sustenance for other organisms and contributing to the overall health of the marine environment.

The Mysterious Aye-Aye

Aye-ayes, Lemur's native to Madagascar, have a long, thin middle finger that they use to tap on tree bark, listening for hollow sound chambers created by insect larvae.

Once they locate a potential meal, they use their specialized elongated incisors to gnaw through the wood and extract the insects, making them uniquely adapted for their niche as nocturnal insectivores.

The Quirky Dung Beetle: Dung beetles play a crucial role in ecosystems by recycling nutrients and organic matter through their consumption of dung, which they roll into balls and bury underground for feeding and reproduction. To navigate efficiently, dung beetles use the sun, moon, and Milky Way as celestial cues, ensuring that they roll their dung balls in a straight line away from competitors and potential predators.

The Amazing Pistol Shrimp: Pistol shrimp, also known as snapping shrimp, possess a specialized claw that can close with incredible speed, creating a cavitation bubble and producing a shockwave that stuns prey or rivals. This shockwave reaches temperatures hotter than the surface of the sun and is powerful enough to disrupt fish schools and deter larger predators, making pistol shrimp formidable hunters.

Vampire Finches' Blood-Feeding Behavior: Vampire finches, native to the Galápagos Islands, exhibit a unique behavior where they peck at the skin of larger birds, to drink their blood. This parasitic behavior provides the finches with additional nutrients, particularly during periods of food scarcity on the islands.

The Unbelievable Immortal Jellyfish: Turritopsis dohrnii, also known as the immortal jellyfish, possesses a unique ability to revert its cells back to a juvenile state after reaching maturity, effectively resetting its biological clock, and potentially achieving indefinite longevity. This process, known as trans differentiation, allows the jellyfish to regenerate damaged tissues and organs and represents an extraordinary example of biological immortality in the animal kingdom.

The Fascinating Glass Frog: Glass frogs, found in Central and South America, have translucent skin that makes their internal organs, including their beating heart and digestive tract, visible from the outside. This transparency is believed to be an adaptation for camouflage, allowing glass frogs to blend in with their leafy surroundings and evade detection by predators.

The Peculiar Mimic Octopus

Mimic octopuses, found in the waters of Southeast Asia, possess an extraordinary talent for imitating other marine creatures, showcasing a level of mimicry unparalleled in the animal kingdom. These cephalopods can mimic not only the appearance but also the behavior of various marine species, including venomous predators like lionfish and sea snakes. Their ability to rapidly change color, shape, and movement allows them to seamlessly blend into their surroundings, effectively camouflaging themselves from both predators and prey. This remarkable adaptation serves as a testament to the mimic octopus's ingenuity and survival instincts in the dynamic and often perilous underwater environment. By mimicking the appearance of potential threats, they deter would-be predators while also ambushing unsuspecting prey, highlighting the intricate strategies employed by marine life to thrive in their natural habitat.

Groundbreaking Medical Breakthroughs

Fecal Microbiota Transplantation (FMT): FMT involves transferring fecal matter from a healthy donor to a recipient with a gastrointestinal condition, such as Clostridium difficile infection, to restore the balance of gut bacteria. This unconventional treatment has shown remarkable success rates, often curing infections that were resistant to standard antibiotics.

Heart Transplant Milestone: In 1967, South African surgeon Christiaan Barnard performed the world's first successful human-to-human heart transplant, transplanting the heart of a deceased donor into a patient with end-stage heart disease. This groundbreaking procedure marked a significant advancement in cardiac surgery and offered hope to patients with previously untreatable heart conditions.

Deep Brain Stimulation (DBS) for Treatment-Resistant Depression: DBS involves implanting electrodes in specific regions of the brain and delivering electrical impulses to modulate abnormal neural activity associated with depression. Despite its unconventional approach, DBS has shown promising results in alleviating symptoms of severe depression in patients who are resistant to other forms of treatment.

Vagus Nerve Stimulation (VNS) for Treatment of Epilepsy: VNS is a surgical procedure that involves implanting a device in the chest to stimulate the vagus nerve, which can help reduce the frequency and severity of epileptic seizures. This innovative therapy offers an alternative for patients who do not respond to traditional anti-seizure medications.

Gene Therapy for Inherited Blindness: Gene therapy for inherited retinal diseases involves delivering functional copies of defective genes to the retina using viral vectors, restoring vision in patients with conditions such as Leber congenital amaurosis. While still in its early stages, this groundbreaking treatment holds promise for treating previously incurable forms of blindness.

Ex Vivo Lung Perfusion (EVLP): EVLP is a technique used to evaluate and rehabilitate donor lungs outside of the body before transplantation, improving the quality and viability of organs for transplant. This innovative approach has expanded the pool of viable donor lungs and improved outcomes for patients awaiting lung transplantation.

Nanotechnology for Targeted Drug Delivery: Nanotechnology involves designing tiny particles, known as nanoparticles, to deliver drugs directly to diseased tissues while minimizing side effects on healthy cells. This approach allows for more precise and efficient drug delivery, improving treatment outcomes for conditions such as cancer and cardiovascular disease.

Microbiome-Based Therapies for Skin Disorders: Microbiome-based therapies involve manipulating the balance of microorganisms on the skin to treat conditions such as acne, eczema, and psoriasis. By targeting the skin microbiome, these innovative treatments offer a novel approach to managing chronic skin conditions and promoting skin health.

Optogenetics for Brain Stimulation: Optogenetics involves genetically modifying neurons to make them sensitive to light, allowing researchers to control neural activity with unprecedented precision. This groundbreaking technique has applications in studying and treating neurological disorders such as Parkinson's disease, epilepsy, and depression.

Intragastric Balloon Therapy for Obesity: Intragastric balloon therapy involves placing a silicone balloon in the stomach to promote feelings of fullness and reduce food intake in obese individuals. This nonsurgical approach to weight loss offers an alternative for patients who are not candidates for bariatric surgery or struggle with traditional weight loss methods.

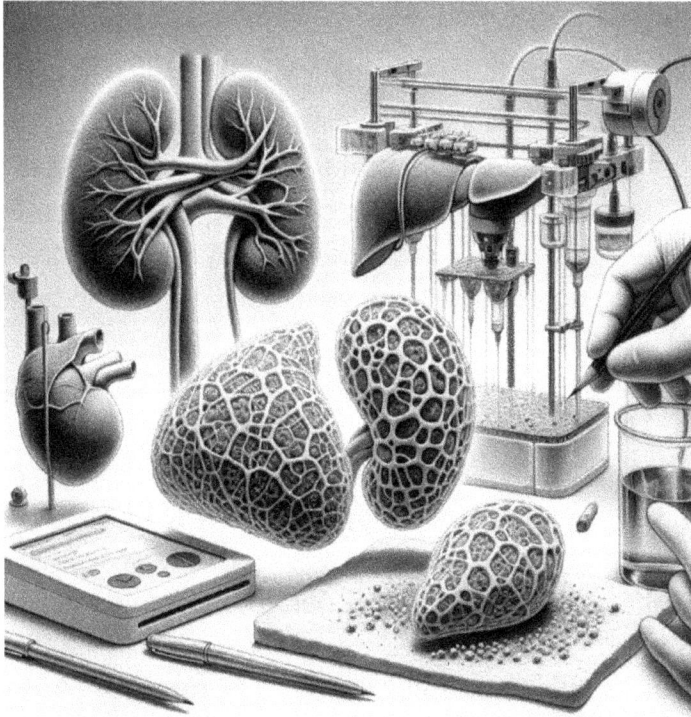

3D-Printed Organs for Transplantation

3D printing technology has enabled the creation of artificial organs, such as kidneys and livers, using a patient's own cells, reducing the risk of organ rejection and the need for immunosuppressive drugs. While still in the experimental stage, 3D-printed organs hold the potential to revolutionize organ transplantation and alleviate the shortage of donor organs. Additionally, 3D-printed organs offer a personalized approach to treatment, as they can be tailored to match the specific anatomical and physiological characteristics of individual patients, improving the success rates of organ transplants, and enhancing patient outcomes.

Artificial Intelligence (AI) for Medical Diagnosis: AI algorithms are increasingly being used to analyze medical images, such as X-rays and MRI scans, to assist radiologists in detecting and diagnosing diseases with greater accuracy and efficiency. This integration of AI into medical practice has the potential to improve diagnostic accuracy, reduce errors, and optimize patient outcomes.

Electroconvulsive Therapy (ECT) for Treatment-Resistant Depression: ECT involves inducing controlled seizures through electrical stimulation of the brain, leading to changes in brain chemistry that alleviate symptoms of severe depression. Despite its controversial history, ECT remains a highly effective treatment for patients who do not respond to medications or psychotherapy.

Transcranial Magnetic Stimulation (TMS) for Treatment of Migraines: TMS is a noninvasive procedure that involves delivering magnetic pulses to specific areas of the brain implicated in migraine pathology, reducing the frequency and severity of migraine attacks. This innovative therapy offers a safe and effective alternative for migraine sufferers who do not respond to conventional treatments.

Intravenous Immunoglobulin (IVIG) Therapy for Autoimmune Disorders: IVIG therapy involves infusing concentrated antibodies derived from healthy donors into patients with autoimmune diseases, such as multiple sclerosis and lupus, to modulate immune responses and reduce inflammation. This immunomodulatory treatment has revolutionized the management of autoimmune disorders, offering relief for patients with debilitating symptoms.

Endoscopic Sleeve Gastroplasty (ESG) for Weight Loss: ESG is a minimally invasive procedure that involves suturing and reshaping the stomach using an endoscope, reducing its capacity, and promoting early satiety. This innovative approach to weight loss offers significant benefits over traditional bariatric surgery, including fewer complications, shorter recovery times, and improved patient satisfaction.

Stem Cell Therapy: Stem cell therapy holds promise for treating a wide range of diseases and injuries by harnessing the regenerative potential of stem cells to repair damaged tissues and organs. From bone marrow transplants for leukemia to experimental treatments for spinal cord injuries and degenerative disorders, stem cell therapy offers hope for patients with previously untreatable conditions.

Intravitreal Injections for Age-Related Macular Degeneration: Intravitreal injections of anti-vascular endothelial growth factor (VEGF) medications have revolutionized the treatment of age-related macular degeneration, a leading cause of blindness in older adults. By targeting abnormal blood vessel growth in the retina, these injections can slow disease progression and preserve vision in patients with this debilitating condition.

Fecal Transplantation for Treatment of Autism Spectrum Disorder (ASD): Emerging research suggests that FMT may have potential therapeutic benefits for individuals with autism spectrum disorder (ASD) by modulating gut microbiota composition and improving gastrointestinal symptoms commonly associated with ASD. While still in its infancy, this unconventional approach holds promise for addressing the underlying gut-brain axis dysfunction implicated in ASD.

The Discovery of Insulin: Canadian scientists Frederick Banting and Charles Best discovered insulin in 1921, revolutionizing the treatment of diabetes. Their groundbreaking work led to the development of insulin therapy, allowing people with diabetes to manage their condition effectively and significantly improving their quality of life.

Mind-Blowing Tech of the Future

Brain-Computer Interfaces (BCIs): BCIs are rapidly evolving, with research focusing on enhancing communication and control for individuals with disabilities. Potential future applications include enabling paralyzed individuals to control robotic prosthetics with their thoughts or facilitating direct brain-to-brain communication.

Quantum Computing: Quantum computers hold the potential to revolutionize fields such as cryptography, materials science, and artificial intelligence. Future quantum computers may solve complex optimization problems, simulate quantum systems with unprecedented accuracy, and accelerate drug discovery processes.

Space Elevators: Space elevators represent a theoretical concept for space transportation, offering a potentially more cost-effective alternative to traditional rocket launches. In the future, space elevators could enable frequent and affordable access to space, facilitating space tourism, satellite deployment, and exploration missions.

Self-Healing Materials: Self-healing materials have promising applications in infrastructure, automotive, and aerospace industries. In the future, self-healing polymers could repair structural damage in buildings or aircraft, while self-repairing electronics could extend the lifespan of consumer devices.

Nanotechnology in Medicine: Future advancements in nanomedicine may lead to targeted drug delivery systems capable of treating diseases at the molecular level. Nanoparticles could be engineered to selectively bind to cancer cells, deliver therapeutic agents, or enhance imaging for early disease detection.

Bioprinting: Bioprinting technology could revolutionize regenerative medicine by fabricating complex tissues and organs for transplantation. In the future, bioprinted organs may alleviate organ shortages, enable personalized medical treatments, and reduce the risk of transplant rejection.

Teleportation

Quantum teleportation research may lead to secure communication networks, quantum internet infrastructure, and novel methods for quantum computing. In the future, teleportation technology could enable instant transmission of quantum information over long distances, advancing fields such as cryptography and quantum entanglement.

Memory Implants: Memory implants could enhance cognitive abilities by providing instant access to vast amounts of information stored in digital databases or cloud networks. In the future, memory enhancement devices may support learning, memory recall, and decision-making processes in everyday life.

Emotion AI: Emotion AI systems may offer personalized services, virtual assistants, and mental health monitoring tools based on real-time analysis of human emotions. Future applications could include AI companions capable of understanding and responding to users' emotional states, improving human-computer interaction and emotional well-being.

Ocean Thermal Energy Conversion (OTEC): OTEC technology has the potential to provide clean, renewable energy from temperature differences in ocean waters. Future OTEC power plants may generate electricity for coastal communities, desalinate seawater, and support sustainable aquaculture practices.

Personalized Medicine: Future advancements in personalized medicine may integrate genomic data, wearable sensors, and artificial intelligence to tailor medical treatments to individuals' unique genetic profiles. Personalized therapies could optimize drug efficacy, minimize side effects, and improve patient outcomes across various diseases and conditions.

Brainwave Authentication: Brainwave authentication systems could offer secure and convenient alternatives to traditional passwords or biometric methods. In the future, brainwave authentication devices may be integrated into wearable technology, smart devices, and cybersecurity systems to enhance data security and user privacy.

Hyperloop Transportation: Hyperloop technology promises to revolutionize long-distance transportation by achieving high speeds in low-pressure tubes. Future hyperloop networks may connect major cities, reducing travel times, congestion, and carbon emissions compared to traditional modes of transportation.

Invisibility Cloaks: While still in the experimental stages, future invisibility cloaks could have applications in military stealth technology, consumer electronics, and medical imaging. Advanced metamaterials may enable the development of adaptive camouflage systems or ultra-thin lenses with enhanced optical properties.

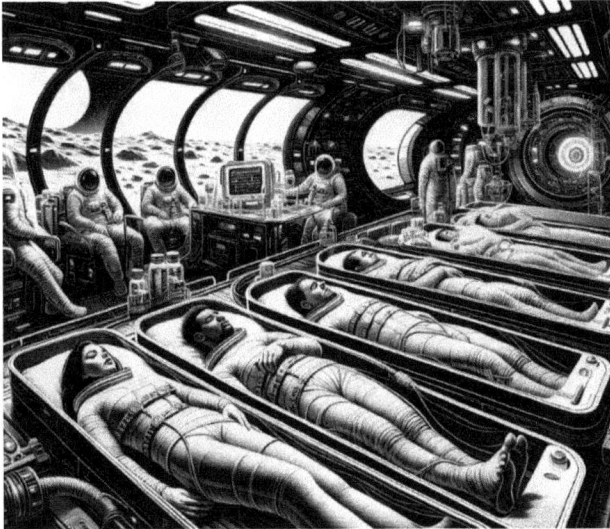

Cryogenic Sleep

Cryogenic sleep research aims to enable long-duration space missions by reducing astronauts' metabolic rates and preserving vital tissues during hibernation. In the future, cryogenic sleep technology may support human exploration of distant planets, asteroids, and exoplanets.

Molecular Assemblers: Molecular assemblers could revolutionize manufacturing by enabling precise control over atomic-scale assembly processes. Future molecular assembly systems may fabricate complex materials, electronics, and pharmaceuticals with unprecedented precision and efficiency.

Artificial Photosynthesis: Artificial photosynthesis holds potential for sustainable energy production by converting sunlight into storable fuels like hydrogen or methanol. Future research may focus on optimizing artificial photosynthetic systems for commercial-scale energy production and reducing reliance on fossil fuels.

Holographic Displays

In addition to entertainment, gaming, and education, future holographic displays hold immense potential for revolutionizing various industries and everyday experiences. With advancements in holographic technology, these displays could find applications in fields such as medicine, where surgeons could visualize complex anatomical structures in three dimensions during procedures, enhancing precision and reducing risks. Furthermore, in architecture and urban planning, holographic displays could enable architects and city planners to visualize and simulate proposed designs in lifelike detail, fostering more informed decision-making and community engagement. As holographic technology continues to evolve, its potential to reshape how we perceive, interact with, and create digital content holds promise for a wide range of applications across diverse sectors.

Remarkable Feats of Engineering

The Palm Islands of Dubai

Dubai's Palm Islands, Palm Jumeirah, Palm Jebel Ali, and Palm Deira, are artificial archipelagos constructed using millions of tons of sand and rock. Shaped like palm trees, these man-made islands are among the largest engineering projects ever undertaken and are visible from space.

The Palm Islands' Coastal Protection Measures: To mitigate erosion and maintain the stability of Dubai's Palm Islands, extensive coastal protection measures were implemented during and after construction. These measures include submerged breakwaters, rock revetments, and beach nourishment programs, demonstrating innovative strategies for sustainable coastal development in urban environments.

The Palm Islands' Marine Habitat Restoration: Despite criticism over environmental impacts, the construction of Dubai's Palm Islands involved extensive efforts to restore and enhance marine habitats. Artificial reefs were created around the islands to promote biodiversity and mitigate the loss of natural ecosystems, showcasing innovative approaches to sustainable development.

The Channel Tunnel's Underwater Alignment: The Channel Tunnel, also known as the Eurotunnel, is a 31-mile underwater rail tunnel connecting England and France beneath the English Channel. Its alignment had to be precisely engineered to accommodate thermal expansion and contraction, tidal movements, and geological conditions, making it one of the most challenging tunneling projects ever undertaken.

The Three Gorges Dam's Resettlement Efforts: The Three Gorges Dam on the Yangtze River in China, the world's largest hydropower project, required the resettlement of over a million people due to flooding caused by the dam's reservoir. Despite criticism over environmental and social impacts, the project showcases the immense engineering feat of controlling one of the world's longest rivers.

The Hoover Dam Bypass Bridge: The Hoover Dam Bypass Bridge, officially known as the Mike O'Callaghan–Pat Tillman Memorial Bridge, spans the Colorado River near the Hoover Dam, providing a vital transportation link between Nevada and Arizona. This impressive bridge features the longest concrete arch span in the Western Hemisphere, showcasing innovative engineering techniques and stunning architectural design.

The Kansai International Airport's Artificial Island: Kansai International Airport in Japan is built on a man-made island in Osaka Bay, making it one of the world's most ambitious airport engineering projects. The island's construction involved extensive land reclamation and innovative engineering techniques to withstand earthquakes, typhoons, and sea level rise.

The Great Wall of China

The Great Wall of China is a testament to ancient engineering ingenuity, constructed primarily during the Qin and Han dynasties and later expanded and reinforced during the Ming dynasty. It consists of various sections built using different materials and techniques, ranging from compacted earth and stone to brick and wood. While some portions of the wall are well-preserved and easily accessible to tourists, others have succumbed to natural erosion and human development over the centuries. Each segment of the wall served a specific strategic purpose, with watchtowers, beacon towers, and fortified passes strategically positioned along its length to provide defense against invading forces. Beyond its military function, the Great Wall also facilitated trade, communication, and the movement of troops and goods across the vast expanse of ancient China. Despite its fame and significance, the Great Wall faced numerous challenges during its construction, including harsh terrain, logistical hurdles, and labor-intensive work, making it one of the most awe-inspiring and enduring engineering marvels in human history.

The Hoover Dam's Concrete Curing Process: The Hoover Dam, built during the Great Depression, required an unprecedented amount of concrete for its construction. To expedite the curing process and prevent cracking, engineers incorporated refrigeration pipes into the concrete blocks, allowing for controlled cooling and ensuring the dam's structural integrity.

The Akashi Kaikyo Bridge's Seismic Isolation: The Akashi Kaikyo Bridge in Japan, the longest suspension bridge in the world, incorporates seismic isolation bearings to protect against earthquakes. These bearings, made of rubber and steel, allow the bridge to absorb and dissipate seismic energy, reducing the risk of structural damage and ensuring passenger safety.

The Burj Khalifa's Foundation: The Burj Khalifa's foundation, consisting of a massive reinforced concrete mat supported by bored piles, is engineered to distribute the tower's weight evenly and prevent settlement. The foundation extends over 50 meters below ground level and is anchored to the bedrock, providing a stable and secure base for the world's tallest building.

The Falkirk Wheel's Water Management System: The Falkirk Wheel's innovative water management system utilizes a balanced hydraulic mechanism to conserve energy and minimize water usage. As boats are transferred between the upper and lower canals, the wheel's interconnected chambers maintain hydraulic equilibrium, allowing water to be recycled and reused with minimal loss, making it one of the most efficient boat lifts in the world.

The Panama Canal's Electrified Locks: The Panama Canal's new set of locks, constructed as part of the canal's expansion project, are powered by an innovative electrohydraulic system. This system uses electric motors to operate the lock gates and fill and empty the lock chambers, improving efficiency and reducing water usage compared to traditional gravity-fed locks.

The Millau Viaduct's Wind Resistance

The Millau Viaduct in France, an architectural marvel, stretches across the Tarn Valley with its sleek and graceful design. Its engineering brilliance lies not just in its aesthetics but also in its ability to withstand the region's harsh weather. The viaduct's innovative design incorporates aerodynamic principles to reduce wind resistance, allowing it to endure powerful gusts that sweep through the valley. Additionally, the viaduct's flexible deck structure enables it to adapt to the dynamic forces exerted by strong winds, ensuring that it remains stable and secure for vehicles traversing its towering height. This combination of form and function makes the Millau Viaduct not only a breathtaking sight but also a testament to human ingenuity in overcoming the challenges of nature.

The Burj Khalifa's Vertical Transportation: The Burj Khalifa in Dubai, the tallest building in the world, features a sophisticated vertical transportation system that includes high-speed elevators and double-decker lifts. These elevators can travel at speeds of up to 40 miles per hour, allowing occupants to reach the top floors in less than a minute.

The Tokyo Skytree's Earthquake Resistance: The Tokyo Skytree, one of the tallest towers in the world, is designed to withstand earthquakes with magnitudes of up to 7.0 on the Richter scale. Its innovative seismic damping system, including a central core with oil dampers, helps dissipate seismic energy and minimize sway during earthquakes.

The Panama Canal's Floating Locks: The Panama Canal, connecting the Atlantic and Pacific Oceans, features a set of unique floating locks at Gatun Lake. These locks, made of hollow concrete chambers, allow ships to transit through the canal by floating on water instead of being lifted and lowered by traditional lock gates. The floating locks at Gatun Lake in the Panama Canal not only facilitate the passage of ships but also mitigate the environmental impact of conventional lock systems by reducing water usage and minimizing disruptions to local ecosystems, showcasing innovative engineering solutions to complex maritime challenges.

The London Crossrail Project's Tunneling Machines: The London Crossrail project, one of the largest infrastructure projects in Europe, employed cutting-edge tunnel boring machines (TBMs) to excavate underground tunnels beneath the city. These massive machines, equipped with rotating cutter heads and conveyor systems, allowed for the rapid and precise construction of tunnels while minimizing disruption to the city above.

Groundbreaking Space Discoveries

The Wow! Signal: Detected on August 15, 1977, by astronomer Jerry R. Ehman during a SETI project, the Wow! Signal remains one of the most intriguing potential signs of extraterrestrial intelligence. Spanning the frequency range of 1420.356 MHz, it lasted for 72 seconds, matching the frequency of the hydrogen line, leading some to speculate it could be a sign of alien communication. However, despite numerous attempts to detect a repeat signal or identify its source, the Wow! Signal has never been conclusively explained, leaving astronomers puzzled and intrigued.

The Pioneer Anomaly: First noticed in the trajectories of the Pioneer 10 and Pioneer 11 spacecraft as they traveled beyond the solar system, the Pioneer Anomaly referred to a slight, unexplained acceleration toward the Sun. Despite exhaustive investigations, including considering thermal radiation and gravitational anomalies, the exact cause remained elusive. Some proposed explanations included uneven heat emission from the spacecraft's surfaces or new physics beyond the laws of gravity, sparking debate among scientists.

Fast Radio Bursts (FRBs): FRBs are brief, intense bursts of radio waves lasting milliseconds, originating from distant galaxies. While astronomers have detected hundreds of these enigmatic signals, their origins remain uncertain. Some theories suggest cataclysmic events such as neutron star mergers or magnetars, while others speculate on artificial sources like alien technology. The continued discovery of FRBs challenges our understanding of astrophysics and the universe's most energetic phenomena.

Tabby's Star: Named after astronomer Tabetha Boyajian, Tabby's Star, also known as KIC 8462852, exhibited irregular and extreme dimming patterns captured by the Kepler Space Telescope. The star's unusual light fluctuations led to speculation about alien megastructures, such as Dyson spheres, causing the dimming. However, subsequent observations and analyses have proposed more natural explanations, including dust clouds or disintegrating comets, while the mystery surrounding Tabby's Star continues to captivate astronomers.

The Great Attractor: The Great Attractor is a gravitational anomaly located in the region of the Hydra-Centaurus Supercluster, drawing galaxies toward it at high speeds. Despite its profound influence on the local universe's motion, the exact nature of the Great Attractor remains obscured by the Milky Way's dust and stars, hindering direct observations. However, ongoing studies using alternative methods such as infrared and radio observations aim to unravel its mysteries and elucidate its role in shaping cosmic large-scale structure.

Dark Matter Filaments: Dark matter filaments are vast, invisible structures that connect galaxies in a cosmic web-like network. These filaments, composed of elusive dark matter, exert gravitational influence on visible matter, shaping the distribution of galaxies across the universe. While dark matter remains undetectable by conventional means, its presence is inferred through its gravitational effects, providing crucial insights into the universe's underlying structure and evolution.

Fermi Bubbles: The Fermi Bubbles are enormous structures extending above and below the plane of the Milky Way galaxy, emitting gamma-ray radiation. While their origin remains uncertain, hypotheses include energetic outflows from the galaxy's central black hole or the remnants of past cosmic events.

The Local Void: The Local Void is a vast region of relatively empty space in the vicinity of the Milky Way galaxy. Its low density of galaxies contrasts with the surrounding cosmic structures, offering insights into the distribution of matter in the universe and the dynamics of cosmic voids.

The Magellanic Stream

The Magellanic Stream is a vast stream of neutral hydrogen gas extending from the Large and Small Magellanic Clouds, satellite galaxies of the Milky Way. Stretching over hundreds of thousands of light-years, this cosmic river offers valuable clues about the Magellanic Clouds' interactions with the Milky Way. However, the stream's origin and evolution continue to puzzle astronomers, driving ongoing research into its formation mechanisms.

Lunar Transient Phenomena: Lunar Transient Phenomena (LTP) are transient changes observed on the moon's surface, ranging from flashes of light to temporary glows or mists. These elusive events, reported by astronomers and amateur observers for centuries, defy easy explanation, with proposed causes including meteorite impacts, electrostatic phenomena, or outgassing from lunar regolith. While some LTP may have natural origins, others remain unexplained, prompting continued monitoring and investigation of our nearest celestial neighbor.

Rogue Planets: Rogue planets, also known as interstellar planets or nomad planets, are celestial bodies that wander through space without orbiting a star. These solitary worlds, ejected from their planetary systems by gravitational interactions or stellar encounters, roam the galaxy as cosmic nomads, challenging conventional notions of planetary formation and evolution. While elusive to detect, rogue planets offer tantalizing prospects for astrobiological research and may harbor exotic environments beyond the confines of traditional habitable zones.

The Cosmic Microwave Background Cold Spot: The Cold Spot is a mysterious and unusually cold region observed in the cosmic microwave background radiation (CMB), the afterglow of the Big Bang. Spanning hundreds of millions of light-years, this cosmic anomaly challenges standard cosmological models and has sparked speculation about exotic phenomena, including collisions with parallel universes or the imprint of cosmic voids. While astronomers continue to study the Cold Spot's properties, its origins remain a subject of ongoing investigation and debate.

The Local Void: The Local Void is a vast, empty region of space surrounding the Milky Way, devoid of galaxies and cosmic structures. Spanning tens of millions of light-years, this cosmic void presents astronomers with a unique opportunity to study the effects of cosmic expansion and large-scale structure on the distribution of galaxies. While the Local Void's origin and impact on the Milky Way remain subjects of scientific inquiry, its existence underscores the dynamic and complex nature of the cosmos on cosmic scales.

The Hubble Constant Debate: The Hubble Constant, which describes the rate of expansion of the universe, has been a subject of ongoing debate among astronomers for decades. Measurements of the

Hubble Constant using different techniques yield slightly different results, leading to discrepancies between observations of the early and late universe. Resolving this discrepancy is crucial for refining our understanding of cosmic evolution, the nature of dark energy, and the fundamental properties of the universe.

The Orphan Stars of Hypervelocity Stars: Hypervelocity stars are celestial objects ejected from galaxies at extreme speeds, propelled by gravitational interactions with supermassive black holes or stellar collisions. Some of these hypervelocity stars become cosmic orphans, wandering through intergalactic space without being bound to any galaxy. Their journeys offer valuable insights into galactic dynamics and interactions, shedding light on the processes that shape the evolution of galaxies and their populations of stars.

The Eridanus Supervoid: The Eridanus Supervoid is one of the largest cosmic voids observed in the universe, spanning hundreds of millions of light-years. Situated in the constellation Eridanus, this vast region of space contains far fewer galaxies and matter than surrounding areas, presenting a significant challenge to cosmological models of structure formation. While its exact origins and implications remain uncertain, the Eridanus Supervoid offers valuable insights into the universe's large-scale structure and evolution.

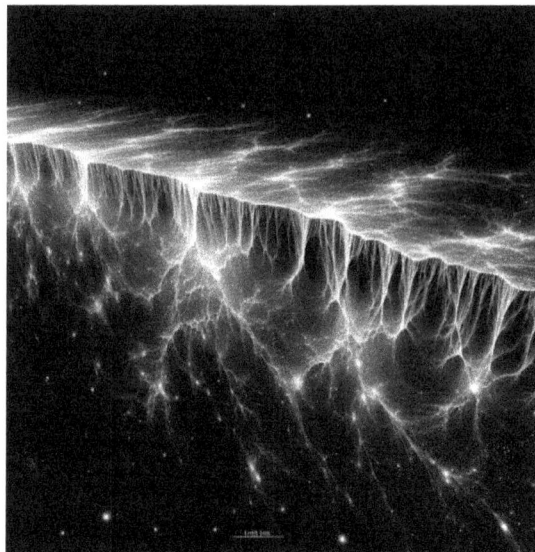

The Great Wall

The Great Wall is one of the largest-known cosmic structures, stretching across billions of light-years, and containing thousands of galaxies. Composed of vast filaments and voids, the Great Wall provides a stunning visual representation of the cosmic web, the large-scale structure of the universe shaped by gravity and dark matter. Its existence challenges cosmological models and offers clues about the universe's origins.

The Gerasimovich–Petukhov Asteroid Belt: The Gerasimovich–Petukhov Asteroid Belt is a recently discovered population of small celestial bodies located beyond the orbit of Neptune. Unlike traditional asteroid belts found within planetary systems, this distant asteroid belt features objects with highly inclined and eccentric orbits, suggesting the presence of unseen perturbing forces shaping the outer solar system's dynamics. Studying the Gerasimovich–

Petukhov Asteroid Belt offers valuable insights into the solar system's formation and evolution, as well as the dynamics of distant celestial objects beyond the realm of traditional planetary systems.

The Kuiper Belt Object Haumea

Haumea is a dwarf planet located in the Kuiper Belt, a region beyond Neptune populated by icy bodies and dwarf planets. Named after the Hawaiian goddess of childbirth, Haumea is notable for its highly rapid rotation, completing a full rotation in just under four hours. Haumea's elongated shape, resembling a flattened ellipsoid, distinguishes it from other dwarf planets and underscores the dynamic processes shaping celestial bodies in the outer solar system. Its rapid rotation not only contributes to its peculiar shape but also generates a pronounced equatorial ridge, hinting at its violent past involving collisions and gravitational interactions. The discovery of Haumea has sparked renewed interest in the Kuiper Belt and prompted further exploration to uncover the mysteries of this distant region, offering clues to the origins and evolution of our solar system. Its discovery in 2004 shed light on the diversity of celestial bodies in the outer solar system and their complex orbital dynamics, providing valuable insights into planetary formation and evolution.

Famous Artifacts and Their Stories

The Shroud of Turin

The Shroud of Turin has captivated the world for centuries, with its enigmatic image of a man bearing wounds consistent with crucifixion. Scientists have conducted various tests on the cloth, including carbon dating, which yielded conflicting results and only added to the mystery surrounding its origins. Some researchers propose that the image was formed through natural processes such as contact with a human body, while others argue for a supernatural explanation, deepening the intrigue and controversy surrounding the artifact.

The Codex Gigas: The Codex Gigas, also known as the Devil's Bible, is a massive medieval manuscript containing religious texts, legends, and illustrations. Legend has it that the entire manuscript was written by a single monk in a single night, with the Devil's help, leading to its eerie reputation and enduring fascination.

The Lost Colony of Roanoke Artifacts: The Lost Colony of Roanoke was an English settlement in present-day North Carolina that mysteriously disappeared in the late 16th century. Despite its enigmatic fate, artifacts discovered in the area, such as pottery shards and metal objects, continue to offer tantalizing clues about the colony's inhabitants and their fate.

The Dead Sea Scrolls: The Dead Sea Scrolls are a collection of ancient Jewish religious texts discovered in caves near the Dead Sea in the mid-20th century. These well-preserved manuscripts shed light on early Jewish religious practices and beliefs, offering valuable insights into the development of Judaism and Christianity.

The Georgia Guidestones: Sometimes referred to as the "American Stonehenge," the Georgia Guidestones are a mysterious monument consisting of four massive granite slabs inscribed with ten guidelines in eight modern languages. Erected in 1980 in rural Georgia, the purpose and origin of the Guidestones remain enigmatic, fueling conspiracy theories and speculation about their true meaning.

The Crystal Skulls: The Crystal Skulls are a collection of quartz crystal skulls believed by some to be ancient Mesoamerican artifacts imbued with supernatural powers. Despite scientific evidence debunking their origins as modern forgeries, the crystal skulls continue to captivate the public imagination with their mysterious allure and alleged mystical properties.

The Elgin Marbles: The Elgin Marbles are a collection of ancient Greek sculptures removed from the Parthenon in Athens by Lord Elgin in the early 19th century. Their acquisition and display in the British Museum have sparked controversy and debate over issues of cultural heritage and ownership, with Greece advocating for their repatriation.

The Terracotta Army

The Terracotta Army is a collection of life-sized clay statues buried near the mausoleum of the first Emperor of China, Qin Shi Huang. Discovered in 1974, the army consists of thousands of intricately crafted soldiers, horses, and chariots, intended to accompany the emperor into the afterlife and protect him in eternity. The sheer scale and attention to detail of the clay statues, estimated to number around 8,000 soldiers, 130 chariots, and 670 horses, attest to the monumental efforts and resources invested in Qin Shi Huang's afterlife preparations. Each soldier in the army is uniquely crafted, with distinct facial features, hairstyles, and armor, reflecting the diverse ranks and roles within the ancient Chinese military hierarchy. The excavation of the Terracotta Army continues to yield new discoveries and insights into the rituals, beliefs, and artistic achievements of the Qin Dynasty, providing a vivid glimpse into the ancient past of China's first imperial dynasty.

The Sumerian King List: The Sumerian King List is an ancient Mesopotamian text detailing the reigns of kings and dynasties from Sumerian history. Containing mythical and historical elements, the list provides a fascinating glimpse into the ancient Sumerian worldview and political structures.

The Emerald Tablet: The Emerald Tablet is a legendary alchemical text attributed to Hermes Trismegistus, the mythical father of alchemy. Said to contain the secrets of transmutation and the philosopher's stone, the tablet has inspired alchemists and occultists throughout history in their quest for spiritual enlightenment and material transformation.

The Book of Kells: The Book of Kells is an illuminated manuscript containing the four Gospels of the New Testament, created by monks in medieval Ireland. Renowned for its intricate illustrations and decorative motifs, the Book of Kells is considered one of the greatest masterpieces of Western calligraphy and religious art.

The Kensington Runestone: The Kensington Runestone is a slab of stone discovered in Minnesota in 1898, inscribed with Scandinavian runes. Despite controversy and skepticism surrounding its authenticity, some believe it to be evidence of pre-Columbian Scandinavian exploration of North America in the 14th century. Furthermore, the Kensington Runestone has sparked debates among historians and archaeologists, with some arguing that it provides compelling evidence of early Norse presence in North America, while others dismiss it as a hoax or misinterpretation.

The Copper Scroll: The Copper Scroll is one of the Dead Sea Scrolls discovered in Qumran, Israel, in the mid-20th century. Unlike other scrolls containing religious texts, the Copper Scroll lists hidden treasures and valuable artifacts, sparking speculation and treasure hunts in search of its elusive treasures.

The Antikythera Mechanism

The Antikythera Mechanism is an ancient Greek device discovered in a shipwreck off the coast of the island of Antikythera. Dating back to the 2nd century BCE, this sophisticated mechanical calculator was used to predict astronomical positions and eclipses, showcasing the advanced scientific knowledge of ancient civilizations. The discovery of the Antikythera Mechanism in 1901 by Greek sponge divers revolutionized our understanding of ancient technology and scientific prowess. The intricate gears and inscriptions on the mechanism's fragments reveal a level of engineering sophistication previously unknown in the ancient world. Researchers believe that the Antikythera Mechanism was designed to track the movements of celestial bodies, including the positions of the sun, moon, and planets, as well as predict astronomical events such as lunar and solar eclipses. Its complexity suggests that it was likely the work of skilled craftsmen and mathematicians, underscoring the advanced knowledge and ingenuity of ancient Greek civilization. The Antikythera Mechanism represents a unique intersection of astronomy, mathematics, and mechanical engineering, offering valuable insights into the intellectual achievements of antiquity and the evolution of scientific thought.

The Baghdad Battery: The Baghdad Battery is a set of ancient artifacts discovered in Iraq that resemble galvanic cells capable of generating electricity. While their exact purpose remains a subject of debate among historians and archaeologists, some speculate that they may have been used for electroplating or medicinal purposes in ancient Mesopotamia.

The Ark of the Covenant

The Ark of the Covenant stands as one of the most iconic and mysterious artifacts in religious history, revered for its role in the Old Testament and its purported divine powers. According to biblical accounts, the ark was constructed at the command of God and housed the stone tablets inscribed with the Ten Commandments given to Moses. Its significance to the Israelites was profound, as it symbolized the covenant between God and his chosen people. Legend has it that the ark possessed supernatural powers, capable of bringing both blessings and calamity to those who encountered it.

Tales from the Animal Kingdom

The Immortal Jellyfish: Turritopsis Dohrnii, also known as the immortal jellyfish, has the remarkable ability to revert to its juvenile polyp stage after reaching maturity, effectively restarting its life cycle. This biological phenomenon allows the jellyfish to potentially live indefinitely, making it one of the only known cases of natural immortality in the animal kingdom.

The Bizarre Courtship Rituals of Bowerbirds: Male bowerbirds engage in elaborate courtship displays to attract mates, building intricate bowers adorned with a variety of objects, including colorful feathers, shells, and even human-made items like bottle caps and plastic toys. These decorative structures serve as stages for the males to perform intricate dances and vocalizations, showcasing their creativity and prowess as mates in the competitive world of bowerbird courtship.

The Bolas Spider: This spider species, mainly found in the Americas and parts of Africa, secretes a special adhesive substance onto its silk, enhancing its stickiness. When the bolas spider detects the vibrations of flying insects nearby, it swings the silk strand, mimicking the motion of a bolas, a South American hunting weapon. Once the silk contacts its target, the sticky substance quickly adheres to the insect, allowing the spider to reel in its catch and consume it at its leisure. This unique hunting technique demonstrates the remarkable diversity of strategies that have evolved in the animal kingdom for survival and sustenance.

The Incredible Journey of the Arctic Tern: The Arctic tern holds the record for the longest migration of any animal, traveling from its breeding grounds in the Arctic to its wintering grounds in the Antarctic and back again, covering a round-trip distance of up to 71,000 kilometers (44,000 miles) annually. This epic journey takes the Tern across every continent and through multiple climate zones, showcasing its remarkable navigational skills and endurance.

The Satanic Leaf-Tailed Gecko's Camouflage

The satanic leaf-tailed gecko, native to Madagascar, possesses remarkable camouflage abilities, allowing it to blend seamlessly into its leafy habitat. With its leaf-like body shape, cryptic coloration, and ability to mimic a dead leaf's texture, this gecko is a master of disguise and an elusive sight in the dense rainforests where it resides. This species takes camouflage to the next level by adopting specific body positions that mimic the appearance of a decaying leaf, complete with browning edges and irregular shapes. Furthermore, its eyes are uniquely adapted to provide excellent night vision, enhancing its ability to remain hidden and avoid detection by predators or prey alike. Such extraordinary adaptations showcase the incredible diversity of evolutionary strategies found within the animal kingdom, particularly in specialized niches like the rainforests of Madagascar.

The Bizarre Behavior of the Cuckoo Bird: Cuckoo birds are notorious for their brood parasitism behavior, laying their eggs in the nests of other bird species and relying on them to raise their young. Some cuckoo species have evolved to mimic the eggs of their host species, ensuring that their eggs are accepted and cared for alongside those of the host, showcasing the cunning strategies employed by these avian impostors.

The Bizarre Mating Habits of Anglerfish: Male anglerfish are much smaller than females and possess specialized olfactory organs for detecting pheromones released by females. Upon finding a female, the male anglerfish latches onto her body with his teeth and eventually fuses with her, sharing a circulatory system and providing sperm whenever she is ready to spawn, showcasing one of the most extreme examples of sexual dimorphism and parasitic mating behavior in the animal kingdom.

The Draco Lizard: In the forests of Southeast Asia, the Draco lizard, also known as the flying dragon, possesses wing-like membranes connected to its elongated ribs, allowing it to glide gracefully between trees. Despite lacking the ability to sustain powered flight, these lizards can glide up to 25 meters between branches, demonstrating remarkable aerodynamic capabilities that aid in predator evasion and territory exploration.

The Surprising Intelligence of Cephalopods: Cephalopods, including octopuses, squid, and cuttlefish, are renowned for their exceptional intelligence, problem-solving abilities, and complex behaviors. From opening jars and solving mazes to displaying sophisticated hunting tactics and even engaging in play, these enigmatic creatures continue to surprise researchers with their cognitive capabilities and adaptability to diverse environments.

The Indestructible Tardigrade

Tardigrades, also known as water bears, are microscopic animals renowned for their ability to survive extreme conditions, including high levels of radiation, extreme temperatures, and even the vacuum of space.

These resilient creatures can enter a state of cryptobiosis, effectively shutting down their metabolism and forming a protective tun, allowing them to endure harsh environments that would be lethal to most other organisms.

The Pistol Shrimp's Sonic Weapon: The pistol shrimp possesses an extraordinary ability to generate a high-speed water jet by snapping its specialized claw shut. This action creates a cavitation bubble that collapses with immense force, producing a loud snapping sound and stunning nearby prey, making the pistol shrimp one of the animal kingdom's most proficient hunters.

The Amazing Ant Mill Phenomenon

Ant mills, also known as death spirals or ant circles, occur when a group of ants becomes trapped in a continuous loop of individuals following one another in a circle until they die from exhaustion or dehydration. This bizarre behavior, observed in some ant species, is thought to be triggered by pheromone trails and can lead to the demise of entire colonies in a phenomenon both fascinating and tragic.

The Ferocious Jaws of the Trap-Jaw Ant: Trap-jaw ants possess some of the fastest mandibles in the animal kingdom, capable of closing their jaws at speeds of up to 230 kilometers per hour (143 miles per hour). These lightning-fast jaws are used for catching prey, launching the ants into the air to escape, and even propelling seeds away from the nest, demonstrating the versatility of this remarkable adaptation.

The Eerie Glow of the Ghostly Octopus: The gliding octopus, also known as the ghost octopus, is a deep-sea species capable of emitting a mesmerizing bioluminescent glow. This eerie display is thought to serve as a form of camouflage or communication in the dark depths of the ocean, where traditional visual cues are scarce, highlighting the fascinating adaptations of marine life to extreme environments.

The Mantis Shrimp's Super Vision: Mantis shrimp have some of the most complex eyes in the animal kingdom, with a unique ability to perceive polarized light and a wide spectrum of colors, including ultraviolet. This remarkable visual acuity enables mantis shrimp to detect prey, communicate with conspecifics, and navigate their vibrant coral reef habitats with unparalleled precision.

The Electric Eel's Shocking Abilities: Electric eels, native to South America, possess specialized organs capable of generating electrical discharges of up to 600 volts, used for both hunting prey and self-defense. This powerful electric shock can incapacitate small fish and deter larger predators, highlighting the eel's unique adaptation for survival in its freshwater habitats.

The Archerfish: Archer fish found in Southeast Asia and Australia, have a unique hunting strategy where they shoot down prey with powerful jets of water expelled from its mouth. These fish have incredibly accurate aim and can adjust the force and trajectory of their water jets to knock insects off overhanging branches, providing a remarkable example of precision hunting in the animal kingdom.

The Enigmatic Platypus: The platypus is a truly unique mammal, native to Australia, known for its duck-like bill, webbed feet, and ability to lay eggs despite being a mammal. This bizarre combination of features puzzled early European naturalists, leading to speculation about the platypus being a hoax or a taxidermist's creation until live specimens were eventually brought to Europe.

Secrets of the Deep Ocean

Bioluminescent Vampire Squid: The vampire squid (Vampyroteuthis infernalis) is a deep-sea cephalopod that inhabits the oxygen minimum zone, where oxygen levels are extremely low. Despite its name, the vampire squid does not feed on blood; instead, it captures marine snow and small organic particles using long, filamentous structures called filaments, emitting a bioluminescent glow to deter predators.

Methane Ice Worms: Methane ice worms (Hesiocaeca methanicola) are species of annelid worms found in methane seeps on the ocean floor, where methane gas escapes from subterranean reservoirs. These worms have evolved specialized adaptations to thrive in extreme conditions, such as high methane concentrations and low temperatures, making them unique inhabitants of the deep sea.

Hydrothermal Vent Communities: Hydrothermal vents are deep-sea ecosystems formed by volcanic activity on the ocean floor, where superheated water rich in minerals gushes from beneath the Earth's crust. These vents support diverse communities of organisms, including giant tube worms, vent crabs, and microbial mats, which rely on chemosynthesis rather than photosynthesis for energy production.

Deep-Sea Jellyfish Blooms: Deep-sea jellyfish, such as the lion's mane jellyfish (Cyanea capillata), form spectacular blooms in the ocean's depths, consisting of thousands of individuals drifting together in the water column. These jellyfish blooms play important ecological roles, serving as food sources for deep-sea predators and contributing to nutrient cycling in the marine environment.

Deep-Sea Hydrothermal Vents: Hydrothermal vents located along mid-ocean ridges release mineral-rich fluids heated by volcanic activity, creating unique ecosystems that support extremophile organisms adapted to high temperatures and chemical toxicity.

Giant Squid Battles Sperm Whales

Giant squids (Architeuthis dux), known for their colossal size and mysterious habits, often find themselves locked in dramatic encounters with sperm whales (Physeter macrocephalus), the ocean's apex predators. These epic battles unfold in the dark depths of the ocean, far from human observation, where the colossal squid must deploy its tentacles and razor-sharp beak to fend off the powerful jaws and relentless attacks of the sperm whale. Despite the rarity of witnessing such events firsthand, evidence of these skirmishes emerges in the form of scars found on the bodies of both squids and whales, offering tantalizing glimpses into the ongoing struggle for survival in the abyssal depths. Such encounters underscore the dynamic and often perilous relationships that exist within the mysterious realm of the deep sea, where each creature must rely on its own unique adaptations and strategies to navigate the relentless cycle of predator and prey.

Bioluminescent Deep-Sea Fish: Many deep-sea fish species possess bioluminescent organs that produce light through chemical reactions involving luciferin and luciferase enzymes. These adaptations serve various functions, including camouflage, communication, and attracting prey, allowing these fish to thrive in the darkness of the deep ocean.

Gigantic Squid Eggs: The eggs of giant squids are among the largest known in the animal kingdom, measuring up to 1.2 meters (4 feet) in length. These massive egg capsules, laid in clusters by female squids, provide protection for developing embryos in the deep-sea environment until they hatch into miniature versions of their colossal parents.

Deep-Sea Bioluminescent Blooms: Deep-sea bioluminescent blooms, or "milky seas," occur when vast expanses of the ocean's surface become illuminated by the collective light emitted by billions of bioluminescent microorganisms. While the exact mechanisms behind these phenomena remain poorly understood, they are believed to result from the aggregation of certain bioluminescent bacteria or dinoflagellates.

Bioluminescent "Firefly" Squid: The firefly squid (Watasenia scintillans), native to the waters off the coast of Japan, is renowned for its dazzling bioluminescent displays. During spawning season, millions of firefly squid gather near the surface, emitting pulsating blue-green light from specialized light organs called photophores, creating a mesmerizing spectacle known as the "jewels of the sea."

Giant Isopods: Giant isopods (Bathynomus giganteus) are crustaceans found in the deep ocean, resembling oversized pill bugs. These scavengers feed on the carcasses of dead marine animals that sink to the ocean floor, utilizing their powerful jaws and armored exoskeletons to crack open tough prey.

Cold-Water Coral Reefs

Deep-sea coral reefs, hidden in the depths of the ocean, are marvels of biodiversity and resilience. Unlike their more famous tropical counterparts, which bask in the sunlight of shallow waters, these cold-water corals endure in the darkness, where temperatures plummet and sunlight barely penetrates. Despite these harsh conditions, deep-sea coral reefs create oases of life, providing shelter, food, and breeding grounds for a myriad of creatures, from tiny crustaceans to deep-sea fishes. Their intricate structures serve as vital habitats and hotspots of biological activity, playing essential roles in the ecology and function of the ocean's vast depths.

Deep-Sea Sperm Whales: Sperm whales (Physeter macrocephalus) are deep-diving cetaceans known to dive to depths of over 2,000 meters in search of prey, including deep-sea squid and fish. Their ability to withstand immense pressures and explore the depths of the ocean makes them key players in deep-sea ecosystems oceans.

These resilient microbes have adapted to survive in complete darkness, crushing pressures, and nutrient scarcity, offering insights into the limits of life on Earth.

Deep-Sea Gigantism: Deep-sea gigantism is a phenomenon observed in certain species of marine organisms, such as giant squids and deep-sea isopods, which grow to unusually large sizes compared to their shallow-water counterparts. The exact causes of deep-sea gigantism remain a subject of scientific debate, with hypotheses ranging from reduced predation pressure to increased resource availability.

Manganese Nodules: Manganese nodules are metallic concretions found on the ocean floor, composed primarily of manganese and iron oxides. These nodules form over millions of years through the precipitation of minerals from seawater, and they are of interest for their potential as a future source of rare earth elements and other valuable minerals.

Deep-Sea "Black Smokers": "Black smokers" are hydrothermal vents characterized by high-temperature, mineral-rich fluid emissions that appear dark due to the precipitation of metal sulfides. These vents support unique ecosystems dominated by chemosynthetic bacteria and specialized organisms adapted to extreme temperatures and chemical conditions.

Bioluminescent Anglerfish: Deep-sea anglerfish, such as the female of the species Ceratiidae, possess a unique bioluminescent lure protruding from their heads, which they use to attract prey in the darkness of the abyssal zone. These bizarre-looking fish demonstrate remarkable adaptations to life in the deep ocean, where food is scarce, and visibility is limited.

Deep-Sea Archaea: Archaea, a type of single-celled microorganism, are abundant in the deep ocean and play crucial roles in biogeochemical cycles, including carbon and nitrogen cycling. These ancient microbes thrive in extreme environments such as hydrothermal vents and cold seeps, where they harness chemical energy to sustain life in the absence of sunlight.

Deep-Sea Luminous Shrimp

Certain species of deep-sea shrimp, such as the Acanthephyra purpurea, possess bioluminescent organs on their bodies, enabling them to produce flashes of light to communicate, attract mates, or confuse predators in the darkness of the abyssal zone. They also have specialized pigments that enable them to perceive and differentiate between different wavelengths of light, aiding in their communication and navigation in the dark depths. These adaptations highlight the intricate ways in which deep-sea organisms have evolved to thrive in one of Earth's most extreme environments, where conventional modes of communication and perception are rendered ineffective.

Environmental Marvels

Bioluminescent Bay: Bioluminescent bays, such as Mosquito Bay in Vieques, Puerto Rico, contain microorganisms called dinoflagellates that emit a blue-green glow when disturbed, creating a mesmerizing natural light show at night. These tiny organisms possess light-producing molecules that emit photons when agitated, a defense mechanism against predators. Visitors to these bays can witness the magical phenomenon by kayaking or swimming in the waters, leaving behind trails of glowing water with each movement.

Socotra Island: Socotra, an island off the coast of Yemen, is home to unique and otherworldly plant species found nowhere else on Earth, including the iconic Dragon's Blood Tree, known for its umbrella-like canopy and crimson sap. The island's isolation and diverse landscapes, ranging from arid deserts to lush forests, have led to the evolution of numerous endemic species adapted to the harsh and variable climate. Socotra's distinct flora and fauna make it a biodiversity hotspot and a UNESCO World Heritage site, attracting botanists, biologists, and nature enthusiasts from around the world.

Cocooned Trees: In Pakistan's Sindh province, trees along the banks of the Indus River become encased in shimmering silk cocoons spun by millions of spiders during the annual flooding season. This natural phenomenon, known as "spider rain," occurs when spiders migrate to higher ground to escape rising floodwaters, weaving intricate webs that blanket the trees, transforming them into ethereal and otherworldly sculptures amidst the watery landscape. The phenomenon of "spider rain" not only showcases the resilience and adaptability of these arachnids but also contributes to the ecosystem by providing additional food sources for birds and other predators. Despite its surreal appearance, this natural event plays a vital role in the intricate web of life along the Indus River's floodplains.

Fairy Circles

In the Namib Desert of Southern Africa, circular patches of barren ground known as fairy circles dot the landscape, their origins shrouded in mystery and the subject of scientific debate. These enigmatic formations have puzzled researchers for decades, with theories ranging from underground termite activity to competition for water and nutrients among desert plants. Fairy circles are a testament to the intricate interplay between geological, biological, and environmental factors in shaping Earth's landscapes, offering a glimpse into the complexities of nature's design.

Underwater Waterfall: Off the coast of Mauritius, an optical illusion creates the appearance of an underwater waterfall, where sand and silt cascade down a steep underwater shelf, creating the illusion of water plunging into an abyss. This mesmerizing phenomenon is caused by sand and silt being carried by strong ocean currents and deposited over the edge of the underwater shelf, creating the illusion of a cascading waterfall when viewed from above. The underwater waterfall is a popular tourist attraction, drawing visitors to witness the stunning spectacle and marvel at the wonders of nature.

Door to Hell: The Darvaza Gas Crater in Turkmenistan, known as the "Door to Hell," is a massive crater that has been burning continuously since 1971, fueled by natural gas reserves deliberately set ablaze to prevent the spread of methane gas. This surreal and otherworldly landscape is a testament to the intersection of human activity and natural phenomena, creating a fiery pit that has fascinated scientists, explorers, and travelers from around the world. Despite its harsh and inhospitable conditions, the Door to Hell has become a popular tourist attraction, drawing visitors to witness its mesmerizing flames and surreal glow in the desert night.

Yakushima Forest: Yakushima Island in Japan is home to one of the world's oldest and most pristine temperate rainforests, featuring ancient cedar trees, some over 1,000 years old, and unique ecosystems teeming with biodiversity. This ancient forest, known as Yakusugi Forest, is a UNESCO World Heritage site and a living museum of natural history, offering visitors the opportunity to explore a pristine wilderness virtually unchanged for millennia. Yakushima's lush landscapes, mist-shrouded mountains, and crystal-clear streams make it a haven for hikers, nature lovers, and adventurers seeking solace and inspiration in the heart of nature.

Blood Falls: In Antarctica's McMurdo Dry Valleys, a glacier releases a stream of iron-rich, saline water that appears blood-red against the white ice, giving rise to the aptly named Blood Falls. This striking phenomenon is caused by the oxidation of iron minerals in the subglacial water as it encounters the air, creating a vivid red coloration. Despite its inhospitable environment, Blood Falls supports microbial life adapted to extreme cold and low oxygen levels, providing scientists with valuable insights into life's resilience in harsh conditions.

Stone Forest

The Stone Forest in Yunnan, China, is a surreal landscape of towering limestone formations resembling petrified trees, formed over millions of years through erosion and geological processes. This natural wonderland, known as Shilin in Chinese, features thousands of karst pillars, caves, and arches, sculpted by the forces of wind and water. The area's labyrinthine pathways and hidden caves have inspired tales of wandering spirits and mythical creatures, adding to its mystical allure. Despite its popularity as a tourist destination, the Stone Forest retains an air of mystery and wonder, inviting visitors to explore its intricate formations and ponder the forces of nature that shaped this extraordinary site over millennia.

Glass Beach: Glass Beach in Fort Bragg, California, is famous for its shoreline adorned with colorful sea glass, created from decades of discarded glass bottles worn smooth by the pounding waves and tides. This unique beach is a testament to the resilience of nature, as the relentless forces of wind and water have transformed trash into treasure over time.

Eternal Flame Falls: In New York's Chestnut Ridge Park, Eternal Flame Falls emits a continuous flame from a natural gas vent behind a waterfall, creating a mesmerizing juxtaposition of fire and water in the midst of the forest. This rare and captivating phenomenon is the result of methane gas escaping from underground rock formations and igniting upon contact with the air, creating a flickering flame that burns perpetually behind the cascading water.

Salar de Uyuni: The Salar de Uyuni in Bolivia is the world's largest salt flat, spanning over 10,000 square kilometers and resembling a vast, otherworldly mirror during the rainy season, reflecting the sky with stunning clarity. This natural marvel, formed by the evaporation of prehistoric lakes, creates a surreal and ethereal landscape that stretches to the horizon in all directions. The Salar de Uyuni is not only a breathtaking sight but also a vital source of salt and minerals for local communities, supporting livelihoods and economic activities in the region.

The Great Blue Hole: The Great Blue Hole off the coast of Belize is a massive underwater sinkhole measuring over 300 meters across and 125 meters deep, renowned for its crystal-clear waters and diverse marine life. This natural wonder, formed during past ice ages when sea levels were lower, offers divers the opportunity to explore its deep blue depths and encounter a variety of marine species, including sharks, rays, and colorful coral reefs. The Great Blue Hole is not only a world-class diving destination but also a UNESCO World Heritage site, highlighting its importance as a unique and ecologically significant marine ecosystem.

Devil's Kettle Falls

In Minnesota's Judge C.R. Magney State Park, the enigmatic Devil's Kettle Falls has puzzled scientists and visitors alike for decades. Despite exhaustive efforts to trace the path of the water that disappears into the deep pothole, its destination remains a mystery, defying conventional explanations. Scientists have employed dye tests, GPS trackers, and even dropping in logs and ping-pong balls, yet the water's whereabouts after plunging into the kettle remains unknown. The enduring mystery of Devil's Kettle Falls continues to captivate the imagination, adding an aura of intrigue to this captivating natural phenomenon.

Fly Geyser: The Fly Geyser in Nevada's Black Rock Desert is a vibrant and otherworldly geothermal geyser adorned with colorful mineral deposits, created accidentally during drilling operations in the early 20th century. Over the years, mineral-rich water from geothermal vents has accumulated around the geyser, forming intricate terraces of vibrant hues, including reds, oranges, and greens. Today, the Fly

Geyser is a striking and surreal landscape, attracting photographers, artists, and curious visitors to marvel at its unique beauty and geological origins.

Living Root Bridge

In the northeastern Indian state of Meghalaya, the indigenous Khasi and Jaintia communities have ingeniously harnessed the regenerative power of nature to create stunning living root bridges, a testament to their profound ecological knowledge and resourcefulness. By carefully guiding the aerial roots of Ficus elastica* trees across riverbanks and ravines, these communities have sculpted resilient and sustainable bridges that grow stronger over time. As the roots continue to grow and intertwine, the bridges become increasingly robust, capable of supporting the weight of numerous travelers and even livestock. Beyond their practical utility, these living root bridges serve as enduring symbols of the deep bond between the people of Meghalaya and their natural surroundings, embodying a harmonious relationship that has endured for generations.

Monarch Butterfly Migration: Each year, millions of monarch butterflies undertake an epic migration journey of over 4,000 kilometers from Canada and the United States to central Mexico, where they gather in massive clusters in oyamel fir forests. This extraordinary migration, spanning multiple generations of butterflies, is a testament to the monarch's remarkable navigational abilities and innate instincts. The spectacle of millions of butterflies blanketing the forest canopy is not only a breathtaking sight but also a vital ecological event, contributing to the pollination of plants and the health of ecosystems along their migratory route.

Singing Sand Dunes: Singing sand dunes, such as those found in the Gobi Desert and the Mojave Desert, have long mystified travelers with their eerie and melodious tunes. This phenomenon occurs when the sand grains shift and rub against each other, creating friction that produces distinct low-frequency sounds. Scientists speculate that the unique shape and size of the sand grains, combined with the presence of certain minerals, contribute to the resonant vibrations that give rise to the haunting melodies. Despite extensive research, the exact mechanism behind the singing sand remains elusive, adding to the mystique of these natural wonders and prompting further investigation into the secrets of the desert.

Iconic Movie Trivia

"The Wizard of Oz" Silver Shoes: In the original book "The Wonderful Wizard of Oz" by L. Frank Baum, Dorothy's magical slippers were silver, not ruby as depicted in the famous 1939 film adaptation. The change was made to take advantage of the newly popular Technicolor technology, which showcased vibrant red shoes on screen.

"The Silence of the Lambs" Moth Scene: The famous scene in "The Silence of the Lambs" where Hannibal Lecter stares at Clarice Starling with a moth on his finger was improvised by actor Anthony Hopkins. The moth was not originally part of the scene but flew onto Hopkins' hand during filming, adding an eerie and unforgettable moment to the movie.

"Jurassic Park" T-Rex Roar: The iconic roar of the Tyrannosaurus rex in "Jurassic Park" was created by combining the sounds of a baby elephant, a tiger, and an alligator. The result was a menacing and realistic roar that became one of the most recognizable sounds in cinematic history.

"Psycho" Shower Scene: In Alfred Hitchcock's "Psycho," the infamous shower scene featuring Janet Leigh's character Marion Crane being stabbed to death took seven days to shoot and included 78 camera setups. Despite lasting only three minutes on screen, the scene became one of the most memorable and influential moments in film history.

"The Shining" Typewriter Scene: Jack Nicholson's famous "All work and no play makes Jack a dull boy" scene in "The Shining" was not accomplished with a prop typewriter loaded with pre-written pages. Instead, each page was individually typed by Nicholson's secretary to create an authentic-looking manuscript.

"Star Wars" Opening Crawl: The iconic opening crawl of "Star Wars: Episode IV - A New Hope" was inspired by the Flash Gordon serials of the 1930s, which also featured text scrolling into the distance at the beginning of each episode. To achieve the effect, the text was physically printed onto a long scroll and filmed against a black background.

Titanic" Soundtrack: The haunting melody played by the musicians as the Titanic sank in James Cameron's "Titanic" was "Nearer, My God, to Thee." While there is debate over which version of the hymn the band played, its inclusion in the film added to the emotional impact of the tragic scene.

"Indiana Jones" Snake Scene: In "Raiders of the Lost Ark," Harrison Ford's fear of snakes is mirrored by Indiana Jones' own phobia. However, Ford's reaction to the snakes in the Well of Souls scene was genuine, as he was unaware of the number of live snakes that would be present on set.

"Back to the Future" Casting Changes: Eric Stoltz was originally cast as Marty McFly in "Back to the Future" but was replaced by Michael J. Fox after several weeks of filming. Footage of Stoltz as Marty still exists, but the decision to recast the role was made due to concerns that Stoltz's performance lacked the comedic energy the role required.

"The Godfather" Horse's Head: The horse head used in the infamous "The Godfather" scene where a severed horse head is placed in a movie producer's bed was real. Director Francis Ford Coppola obtained the horse head from a dog food company, ensuring authenticity and adding to the shock value of the scene.

"E.T. the Extra-Terrestrial" Alien Voice: The voice of E.T. in Steven Spielberg's "E.T. The Extra-Terrestrial" was created using a combination of recordings of actress Pat Welsh, who had smoked heavily and had a raspy voice, and sound effects technician Ben Burtt's own vocalizations. The result was a unique and instantly recognizable alien voice that captivated audiences worldwide.

"Casablanca" Final Line: Humphrey Bogart's iconic final line in "Casablanca," "Louis, I think this is the beginning of a beautiful friendship," was ad-libbed during filming. The script originally called for a different ending line, but Bogart's improvisation has since become one of the most memorable lines in cinematic history.

"Jaws" Mechanical Shark: The mechanical shark used in "Jaws" was notoriously unreliable, often malfunctioning due to saltwater exposure and technical issues. As a result, director Steven Spielberg was forced to rely on creative camera techniques and suspenseful music to build tension, leading to the shark being seen less frequently in the film than originally planned.

"Rocky" Original Ending: The original ending of "Rocky" had Sylvester Stallone's character, Rocky Balboa, throwing his final fight against Apollo Creed. However, Stallone fought for a more uplifting ending where Rocky goes the distance and loses the fight but wins the hearts of the audience, ultimately leading to the film's iconic final scene on the steps of the Philadelphia Museum of Art.

"The Matrix" Bullet Time: The groundbreaking "bullet time" effect used in "The Matrix" to depict slow-motion action sequences was achieved using a combination of multiple cameras and computer-generated imagery. The innovative technique revolutionized action filmmaking and inspired countless imitations and parodies in movies and television shows.

"The Exorcist" Curse: Several strange incidents occurred during the filming of "The Exorcist," leading to rumors of a curse surrounding the production. These included set fires, on-set injuries, and even deaths of cast and crew members. While many of these incidents can be attributed to coincidence or natural causes, the "curse" remains a notorious part of the film's legacy.

"The Breakfast Club" Detention: The cast of "The Breakfast Club" spent their off-screen time together in the high school library where most of the film takes place, further bonding and developing their on-screen chemistry. Director John Hughes wanted to foster a sense of camaraderie among the actors, resulting in authentic performances and memorable interactions between the characters.

"Pulp Fiction" Briefcase Contents: The contents of the mysterious briefcase in "Pulp Fiction" are never revealed in the film, leading to speculation and fan theories about its significance. While director Quentin Tarantino has remained coy about the briefcase's contents, he has stated that it represents whatever the viewer wants it to be, adding to the film's enigmatic and open-ended nature.

"The Princess Bride" Fezzik's Size: Andre the Giant, who played the character Fezzik in "The Princess Bride," was so large that Robin Wright, who played Princess Buttercup, often stood on a specially built platform during their scenes together to compensate for the height difference. Despite his imposing size, Andre was known for his gentle nature and sense of humor on set, endearing him to his fellow cast members and crew.

Intriguing World Records

Longest Fingernails: The record for the longest fingernails ever belonged to Lee Redmond from the United States, whose nails measured a total of over 28 feet long before she lost them in a car accident in 2009.

Most Piercings: As of 2022, the record for the most piercings on a single person is held by Brazilian Elaine Davidson, who had a staggering 6,925 piercings all over her body, including 500 in her genitalia.

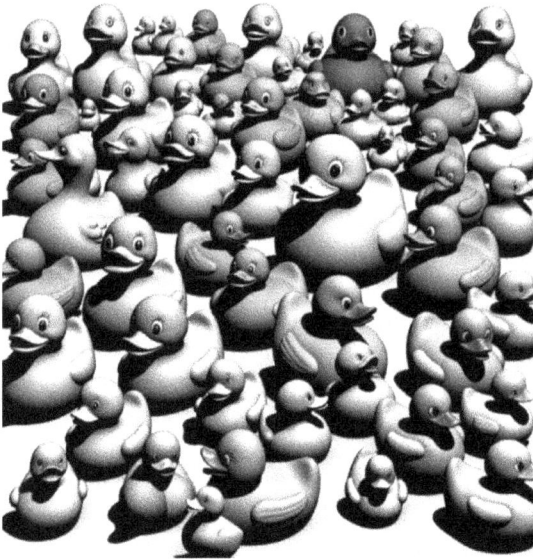

Largest Collection of Rubber Ducks

The largest collection of rubber ducks belongs to Charlotte Lee from the United States, who has amassed over 10,000 rubber ducks of various shapes, sizes, and designs.

Longest Time Spent Playing a Video Game: The record for the longest videogame marathon playing a single game is held by Okan Kaya from Australia, who played Call of Duty: Black Ops 2 for 135 hours and 50 minutes straight in 2012.

Most Big Macs Consumed: The record for the most Big Macs consumed in a lifetime is held by Donald A. Gorske from the United States, who has eaten over 32,000 Big Macs since 1972.

Largest Collection of Smurfs Memorabilia: The largest collection of Smurfs memorabilia belongs to Stephen Parkes from the United Kingdom, who has collected over 11,000 items related to the popular cartoon characters.

Most Tattooed Senior Citizens: Charlotte Guttenberg and Chuck Helmke from the United States hold the record for being the most tattooed senior citizens, with over 90% of their bodies covered in tattoos.

Longest Time Balancing a Lawn Mower on Chin: The record for the longest time balancing a lawn mower on the chin is held by Ashrita Furman from the United States, who balanced a running lawn mower on his chin for 3 minutes and 1 second in 2010.

Largest Collection of Pokémon Memorabilia: Lisa Courtney from the United Kingdom holds the record for the largest collection of Pokémon memorabilia, with over 16,000 items including cards, toys, and clothing.

Most Consecutive Days Riding a Roller Coaster: The record for the most consecutive days riding a roller coaster is held by Richard Rodriguez from the United States, who rode a roller coaster every day for 2,000 consecutive days.

Longest Time Spent Hula Hooping: The record for the longest time spent hula hooping is held by Aaron Hibbs from the United States, who hula hooped for 74 hours and 54 minutes straight in 2009.

Most Pogo Stick Jumps in One Hour: The record for the most pogo stick jumps in one hour is held by James Roumeliotis from Canada, who completed 206,864 jumps in 2011.

Largest Collection of Banana Labels: The largest collection of banana labels belongs to Wally Hedrick from the United States, who has collected over 17,000 labels from bananas all over the world.

Longest Time Spent Standing on Ice: Dutchman Wim Hof, also known as "The Iceman," holds the record for the longest time spent standing in ice, enduring temperatures of -20°C (-4°F) for 1 hour and 53 minutes.

Most Jell-O Eaten with Chopsticks in One Minute: Ashrita Furman holds another unusual record for eating the most Jell-O with chopsticks in one minute, consuming a staggering 170 grams (6 ounces) in 2015.

Largest Collection of Traffic Cones: David Morgan from the United Kingdom holds the record for the largest collection of traffic cones, with over 137 different cones in various shapes, sizes, and colors.

Longest Distance Skateboarded by a Goat: Happie the Goat, owned by Melody Cooke from the United States, holds the record for the longest distance skateboarded by a goat, covering 36 meters (118 feet) in 25 seconds in 2012.

Most Snails on the Face: Fin Kehler from the United States holds the record for the most snails placed on the face at one time, balancing 43 live snails on his face for 10 seconds in 2009.

Largest Collection of Potato Chip Bags: Barry Krider from the United States holds the record for the largest collection of potato chip bags, amassing over 5,000 different bags from around the world.

Most Toilet Seats Broken by the Head in One Minute: Kevin Shelley from the United States holds the record for the most toilet seats broken by the head in one minute, smashing 46 seats with his head in 2007.

Fascinating Facts about the Human Body

Gut Feelings: The enteric nervous system, often referred to as the "second brain," consists of millions of neurons embedded in the walls of the digestive tract. These neurons form a complex network that communicates with the central nervous system and play a crucial role in regulating digestion, immune function, and even mood. Research suggests that disturbances in the gut-brain axis may contribute to conditions like irritable bowel syndrome (IBS) and mood disorders such as anxiety and depression.

Brain Power: The brain's electrical activity arises from the coordinated firing of billions of neurons, which communicate through rapid changes in electrical potentials. This intricate network of neurons forms complex circuits responsible for various cognitive functions, including perception, memory, language, and decision-making. Despite its relatively low power consumption compared to other organs, the brain's computational capacity and efficiency are unparalleled, allowing humans to process vast amounts of information and adapt to diverse environments.

Self-Cleaning Lungs: Cilia are hair-like structures lining the respiratory tract that beat in coordinated waves, moving mucus and trapping particles out of the airways. This mucociliary clearance system acts as a primary defense mechanism against airborne pathogens, pollutants, and debris. In conditions like cystic fibrosis and chronic obstructive pulmonary disease (COPD), dysfunction of the mucociliary clearance system can lead to mucus buildup and respiratory infections.

Endless Nails: The growth rate of fingernails varies among individuals and is influenced by factors such as genetics, age, and overall health. Fingernails typically grow faster than toenails, with an average growth rate of about 1/8 inch per month. However, certain conditions like nail psoriasis and fungal infections can affect nail growth and lead to abnormalities in nail shape and texture.

Tooth Regeneration: Unlike humans, some species of sharks possess a remarkable ability to continuously regenerate their teeth throughout their lives. In sharks, tooth regeneration occurs through the continuous growth and replacement of teeth from specialized structures called tooth files. This adaptive feature enables sharks to maintain functional dentition despite the wear and tear associated with their predatory lifestyle.

Eye Movements: The muscles responsible for moving the eyes—the six extraocular muscles—are among the fastest and most precise in the human body. These muscles work in coordinated pairs to control the movement and alignment of the eyes, allowing for smooth pursuit of moving objects, precise fixation on targets, and rapid shifts in gaze direction. Dysfunction of the extraocular muscles can lead to conditions like strabismus (eye misalignment) and nystagmus (involuntary eye movements).

Muscle Memory: Muscle memory, also known as procedural memory, refers to the ability to perform learned movements and tasks automatically, without conscious effort. This phenomenon is mediated by neural circuits in the brain's motor cortex and basal ganglia, which encode and store information about skilled movements through repeated practice and reinforcement. Activities like playing a musical instrument, typing on a keyboard, or riding a bike rely heavily on muscle memory and can be performed with precision and fluency even after extended periods of disuse.

Superhuman Smell: Hyperosmia, or a heightened sense of smell, can be either congenital (present from birth) or acquired due to factors like hormonal changes, pregnancy, or neurological conditions. Individuals with hyperosmia may experience increased sensitivity to odors, detecting faint scents that others may not notice. While hyperosmia can enhance certain sensory experiences, it can also be overwhelming and disruptive in environments with strong or unpleasant odors.

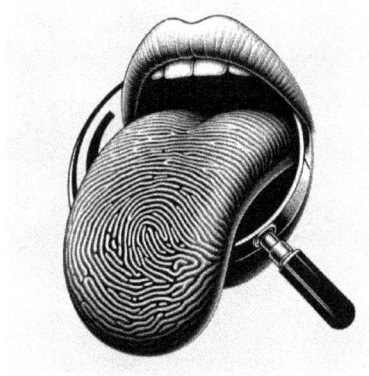

Tongue Print

While fingerprints have been used for identification purposes for over a century, researchers have explored the potential of tongue prints as a unique biometric identifier. Like fingerprints, tongue prints exhibit individualized patterns of ridges and grooves, making them potentially useful for forensic investigations and identity verification. However, the practicality and reliability of tongue prints as a biometric identifier remain subjects of ongoing research and debate.

Skin Shedding: The outer layer of the skin, known as the epidermis, undergoes continuous renewal through a process called desquamation. Skin shedding helps remove dead skin cells, prevent clogging of pores, and maintain the skin's barrier function. Factors such as age, climate, and skincare habits can influence the rate of skin shedding and the overall health and appearance of the skin.

Phantom Limb Sensations: Phantom limb sensations are complex perceptual experiences that occur in individuals who have undergone limb amputation or loss. These sensations can include feelings of itching, tingling, warmth, or pain originating from the missing limb. While the exact mechanisms underlying phantom limb sensations are not fully understood, they are thought to arise from neural reorganization in the brain's somatosensory cortex following limb loss.

Yawning Contagion

Contagious yawning is a well-documented phenomenon characterized by the involuntary urge to yawn when witnessing another person yawning. This contagious behavior is thought to be linked to social bonding.

Hair Growth: Hair growth occurs in three distinct phases: anagen (growth phase), catagen (transitional phase), and telogen (resting phase). The rate and pattern of hair growth are influenced by factors like genetics, age, hormonal fluctuations, nutritional status, and environmental factors. While human hair growth is relatively slow compared to other mammals, it serves essential functions like thermoregulation, protection against ultraviolet (UV) radiation, and sensory perception.

Incredible Flexibility: Flexibility refers to the range of motion around a joint or series of joints and is influenced by factors like muscle elasticity, joint structure, and connective tissue integrity. While some individuals possess innate flexibility due to factors like genetics and joint laxity, others can improve flexibility through regular stretching and mobility exercises. Extreme flexibility, as exhibited by contortionists and gymnasts, requires a combination of genetic predisposition, rigorous training, and specialized conditioning to achieve and maintain.

Brain's Power Consumption: The brain's high energy demand is primarily driven by its extensive network of neurons and glial cells, which require constant metabolic activity to maintain cellular functions and synaptic communication. Despite accounting for only about 2% of the body's weight, the brain consumes approximately 20% of the body's oxygen and glucose supply.

Hiccup Mystery: Hiccups, or singultus, are involuntary contractions of the diaphragm muscle followed by sudden closure of the vocal cords, resulting in the characteristic "hic" sound. While hiccups typically resolve spontaneously within a few minutes, persistent or chronic hiccups lasting for hours or days may indicate underlying medical conditions. Despite numerous theories, the exact cause of hiccups remains uncertain.

Unique Smell: Each person has a distinct body odor, influenced by factors such as genetics, diet, personal hygiene, and microbial activity on the skin. Human body odor is primarily produced by apocrine sweat glands, which secrete odorless substances that bacteria metabolize into volatile compounds responsible for characteristic smells. While body odor is often considered a taboo topic, it plays essential roles in social communication, mate selection, and personal identity.

Blinking: Blinking is a vital physiological process that helps keep the surface of the eye moist, clear away debris, and protect against foreign particles and irritants. The average person blinks approximately 15-20 times per minute, although blink rate can vary depending on factors like concentration, fatigue, and environmental conditions. Blinking also serves non-visual functions, such as signaling emotional states like anxiety, stress, or excitement.

Unusual Cultural Traditions

La Tomatina: In the Spanish town of Buñol, participants engage in an annual festival known as La Tomatina, where they pelt each other with overripe tomatoes in a massive food fight. This bizarre tradition, which originated in the 1940s, attracts thousands of visitors each year and culminates in streets running red with tomato pulp.

The Day of the Dead: In Mexico, families honor deceased loved ones during the Day of the Dead by creating elaborate altars adorned with marigolds, sugar skulls, and favorite foods and beverages of the departed. This colorful and festive tradition, celebrated on November 1st and 2nd, serves as a joyful remembrance of the deceased and a celebration of life.

The Baby Jumping Festival: In Castrillo de Murcia, Spain, locals participate in the Baby Jumping Festival, where men dressed as the devil leap over rows of infants lying on mattresses in the streets. This centuries-old tradition is believed to cleanse the babies of original sin and protect them from evil spirits.

The Wife Carrying World Championships: In Sonkajärvi, Finland, couples from around the world compete in the Wife Carrying World Championships, where male participants race through an obstacle course while carrying their female partners on their backs. This quirky tradition, inspired by Finnish folklore, tests participants' strength, agility, and teamwork in pursuit of victory and bragging rights.

The Thaipusam Festival: In Malaysia and Singapore, devotees of the Hindu deity Murugan participate in the Thaipusam Festival, where they undergo acts of self-mortification as expressions of devotion and penance. Participants pierce their bodies with hooks, skewers, and spears, carry elaborate kavadis (ornate structures), and embark on grueling processions to temples, symbolizing their commitment to faith and spiritual purification.

Cheese Rolling

In Gloucestershire, England, participants gather annually for the Cooper's Hill Cheese-Rolling and Wake, where they chase a wheel of cheese down a steep hillside. Despite the inherent risks of injury, contestants vie for the coveted prize of catching the cheese or simply revel in the exhilarating chaos of the event.

The Running of the Bulls: Each year in Pamplona, Spain, daring participants run through the streets alongside stampeding bulls during the San Fermín festival. This adrenaline-fueled tradition, dating back to the 14th century, tests the bravery and agility of participants as they navigate narrow cobblestone streets in the path of charging bulls.

Boryeong Mud Festival: In South Korea, the Boryeong Mud Festival attracts millions of visitors who indulge in mud-based activities such as mud wrestling, mudslides, and mud baths. This unusual tradition, held annually in Boryeong, celebrates the purported health and beauty benefits of mineral-rich mud.

The Red Rain of Kerala: In Kerala, India, locals celebrate the mysterious phenomenon known as the "Red Rain," where rainfall appears blood-red due to the presence of microscopic algae. This unusual occurrence, first recorded in 2001, continues to puzzle scientists and has sparked various cultural interpretations and superstitions.

Yak Shaving in Mongolia: In Mongolia, the tradition of yak shaving involves a ceremonial shearing of yaks by skilled herders using traditional tools. This ancient practice not only provides essential wool for clothing and insulation but also serves as a communal activity that strengthens social bonds within nomadic communities.

Holi Festival of Colors: In India, the Holi Festival is a vibrant celebration that marks the arrival of spring and the triumph of good over evil. Participants engage in playful revelry, dousing each other with colored powders and water, dancing to lively music, and indulging in festive treats, fostering a sense of unity, joy, and renewal.

Takanakuy Festival (Peru): The Takanakuy Festival, held in the Peruvian Andes, is a unique cultural event where individuals voluntarily engage in physical combat to resolve personal conflicts and grievances. Contrary to promoting violence, the festival is rooted in indigenous traditions aimed at fostering community unity and harmony by allowing participants to confront their issues openly and peacefully. The fights are conducted under strict rules and regulations to ensure safety, and participants often embrace afterward as a symbol of reconciliation, demonstrating the festival's emphasis on resolution rather than aggression.

The Whirling Dervishes of Turkey: The Mevlevi Order in Turkey practices the whirling dervish ritual, where devotees spin in a trance-like state as a form of spiritual meditation and connection with the divine. This mesmerizing tradition, characterized by graceful movements and rhythmic spinning, symbolizes the journey of the soul towards enlightenment and union with the divine.

The Fire Walking Festival

In countries such as Greece, India, and Fiji, the Fire Walking Festival is a sacred ritual where participants walk barefoot over hot coals or embers without sustaining burns. This awe-inspiring tradition, rooted in religious and cultural beliefs, symbolizes purification, protection from harm, and the triumph of faith over fear.

223

The Saturnalia Festival: In ancient Rome, the Saturnalia Festival was a raucous celebration held in honor of the god Saturn, characterized by feasting, drinking, and merrymaking. During this week-long event, social norms were temporarily overturned, with slaves being served by their masters and revelers engaging in uninhibited revelry and revelry.

Gurning Competition (England): Originating in England, gurning competitions involve contestants contorting their faces into grotesque expressions, often by sticking their heads through a horse collar or "Baffin," to amuse spectators and judges.

The Pushkar Camel Fair: In Pushkar, India, the Pushkar Camel Fair is a vibrant cultural event where thousands of camels, horses, and livestock are traded, raced, and adorned with elaborate decorations. This colorful spectacle attracts pilgrims, traders, and tourists from around the world, fostering a festive atmosphere of music, dance, and traditional competitions.

Monkey Buffet Festival: In Lopburi, Thailand, locals host the Monkey Buffet Festival, where they lay out elaborate feasts for thousands of macaque monkeys that inhabit the area. This quirky tradition, held annually to promote tourism and celebrate the bond between humans and monkeys, features colorful fruit displays and playful interactions with the primates.

The Tinku Festival: In Bolivia, the Tinku Festival is an annual ritualistic event where indigenous communities engage in ritualized combat to honor Pachamama, the Earth Mother. Participants, adorned in traditional attire, engage in fierce hand-to-hand combat as an offering to the earth goddess, symbolizing fertility, and prosperity.

Unusual Festivals Around the World

Hadaka Matsuri (Naked Festival): In Japan, Hadaka Matsuri involves thousands of men wearing loincloths competing to grab sacred sticks thrown by a priest, believed to bring good fortune and prosperity for the year ahead.

La Tomatina: Held annually in Buñol, Spain, La Tomatina is a massive tomato fight where participants throw overripe tomatoes at each other, turning the streets into a sea of red pulp.

Songkran Water Festival: Celebrated in Thailand, Songkran marks the traditional Thai New Year with a nationwide water fight, where people drench each other with water guns, buckets, and hoses to symbolize washing away bad luck and sins.

The Golden Shears Shearing and Wool handling Championships: In New Zealand, the Golden Shears Championships showcase the skill and athleticism of sheep shearers and wool handlers from around the world. Competitors shear sheep at lightning speed, aiming for precision and efficiency as they vie for the title of world champion.

Bull Run (San Fermin): The San Fermin festival in Pamplona, Spain, includes the famous Running of the Bulls, where brave participants sprint ahead of charging bulls through the city's streets, risking injury in the name of tradition.

Kanamara Matsuri (Festival of the Steel Phallus): Taking place in Kawasaki, Japan, Kanamara Matsuri celebrates fertility and sexual health with phallic-shaped decorations, candies, and parades, attracting visitors from far and wide.

Wife Carrying World Championship: Held in Sonkajärvi, Finland, the Wife Carrying World Championship challenges male competitors to race through an obstacle course while carrying their female partners on their backs.

Day of the Dead (Dia de los Muertos)

Observed primarily in Mexico but also celebrated in other Latin American countries, the Day of the Dead, or Día de los Muertos, is a vibrant and culturally rich tradition deeply ingrained in the collective identity of the region. Families meticulously prepare for this annual event by meticulously cleaning and decorating the gravesites of their departed relatives, adorning them with marigolds, candles, photographs, and the favorite foods and drinks of the deceased. Altars, known as ofrendas, are meticulously assembled in homes and public spaces, adorned with intricate sugar skulls, papel picado (decorative paper), and symbolic offerings to welcome the spirits of the departed back to the realm of the living. This joyous occasion is not a somber affair but rather a jubilant celebration of life and death, where music, dance, and laughter fill the streets as communities come together to honor their ancestors and celebrate the continuity of family ties across generations.

Up Helly Aa: Held in Lerwick, Scotland, Up Helly Aa is a Viking fire festival where participants dressed as Vikings parade through the streets carrying torches before burning a replica Viking longship in a dramatic display of flames.

Boryeong Mud Festival: South Korea's Boryeong Mud Festival attracts visitors from around the world to frolic in mud pools, compete in mud wrestling, and enjoy mud-based skincare treatments.

Bun Festival: Celebrated on Cheung Chau Island, Hong Kong, the Bun Festival features Taoist rituals, lion dances, and a climbing competition where participants scramble up a tower of buns to retrieve the blessed buns for good luck.

Night of the Radishes (Noche de Rábanos): In Oaxaca, Mexico, the Night of the Radishes is an annual event where artisans carve intricate sculptures out of giant radishes, showcasing their creativity and craftsmanship.

Gion Matsuri: Kyoto's Gion Matsuri is one of Japan's most famous festivals, featuring massive floats adorned with intricate tapestries and decorations paraded through the city's streets in a display of cultural heritage and tradition.

Burning Man: Held in Nevada's Black Rock Desert, Burning Man is an annual gathering where participants create a temporary city in the desert, emphasizing self-expression, community, and radical self-reliance, culminating in the burning of a large wooden effigy.

Pushkar Camel Fair: In Rajasthan, India, the Pushkar Camel Fair is a vibrant event where thousands of camels, horses, and livestock are bought and sold, accompanied by cultural performances, camel races, and traditional competitions.

Chinchilla Melon Festival: Queensland, Australia, hosts the Chinchilla Melon Festival, featuring quirky events like melon skiing, melon bungee, and a melon ironman race, celebrating the region's agricultural heritage in a fun and lighthearted manner.

Wakakusa Yamayaki: In Nara, Japan, the Wakakusa Yamayaki festival culminates in the burning of Mount Wakakusa's grass-covered slopes, creating a spectacular blaze visible from miles around and marking the beginning of the new year.

Thaipusam

Celebrated by Tamil communities worldwide, Thaipusam is a Hindu festival where devotees pierce their bodies with hooks, skewers, and other objects as acts of devotion and penance, demonstrating their faith and endurance in the face of pain and sacrifice.

Holi Festival of Colors: Celebrated in India and Nepal, Holi is a vibrant festival where participants throw colored powder and water at each other to celebrate the arrival of spring and the triumph of good over evil.

Bizarre Foods from Different Cultures

Balut (Philippines): Balut is a popular street food in the Philippines, typically enjoyed with a sprinkle of salt and a dash of vinegar. Despite its appearance of a partially formed duck embryo, balut is prized for its rich flavor and is believed to have aphrodisiac qualities.

Fried Tarantulas (Cambodia): Fried tarantulas are a popular street food in Cambodia, particularly in the town of Skuon. The spiders are typically seasoned with garlic, salt, and sugar, then deep-fried until crispy. Despite their intimidating appearance, fried tarantulas have a crunchy texture and a flavor often compared to crab or chicken.

Surströmming (Sweden): Surströmming, a fermented Baltic herring, is a staple of Swedish cuisine. The herring is caught, fermented in barrels for several months, then canned. Despite its overpowering smell, which has been likened to rotting garbage, surströmming is enjoyed by many Swedes, often eaten with flatbread, potatoes, and onions.

Sannakji (South Korea): Sannakji is a Korean dish of live octopus tentacles, typically seasoned with sesame oil and served immediately after being chopped. The tentacles continue to squirm on the plate, creating a sensation of freshness and texture. Despite potential choking hazards, sannakji is enjoyed for its unique flavor and cultural significance in South Korea.

Century Egg (China): Century eggs, also known as hundred-year eggs or thousand-year eggs, are preserved duck, chicken, or quail eggs. They're coated in a mixture of clay, ash, salt, quicklime, and rice hulls, then left to ferment for several weeks or months. Despite their pungent odor and translucent appearance, century eggs have a rich, creamy yolk and a complex, umami flavor prized in Chinese cuisine.

Cuy (Peru): Cuy, or guinea pig, is a traditional Andean dish dating back to pre-Columbian times. The small rodents are typically roasted whole on a spit or grilled, then served with potatoes and vegetables. Despite their status as pets in many Western countries, cuy is considered a delicacy in Peru, prized for its tender meat and rich flavor.

Casu Marzu (Italy): Casu Marzu, a traditional Sardinian cheese, is made from sheep's milk and left to ferment with live insect larvae of the Piophila casei fly. The larvae break down the cheese's fats, resulting in a soft, spreadable texture and a strong, tangy flavor. While it's considered a delicacy by some, its production is illegal due to health concerns.

Fugu (Japan)

Fugu, or pufferfish, is highly toxic due to the presence of tetrodotoxin in its organs, particularly the liver and ovaries. Skilled chefs undergo rigorous training and licensing to prepare fugu safely, removing the toxic parts while leaving behind the delicious and tender flesh. Despite the risks, fugu is a prized delicacy in Japan, often served raw as sashimi or in hotpot dishes.

Escamoles (Mexico): Escamoles, also known as "insect caviar," are ant larvae harvested from the roots of agave plants in Mexico. Despite their appearance, escamoles have a nutty flavor and creamy texture, like pine nuts or cottage cheese. They're often used in traditional Mexican dishes like tacos or omelets, prized for their unique taste and cultural significance.

Kopi Luwak (Indonesia)

Kopi Luwak, also known as civet coffee, is made from coffee beans that have been eaten, partially digested, and excreted by civet cats. After being collected, cleaned, and roasted, the beans produce a coffee with a unique flavor profile, often described as smooth, earthy, and less bitter than traditional coffee. Despite its high price tag, kopi luwak is enjoyed by coffee connoisseurs around the world.

Khash (Armenia): Khash is a traditional Armenian dish made from boiled cow or sheep's feet, typically seasoned with garlic, salt, and vinegar. It's often served as a warming winter soup, enjoyed with crusty bread and vodka. Despite its simple ingredients, khash is prized for its rich, gelatinous broth, making it a beloved comfort food in Armenia.

Huitlacoche (Mexico): Huitlacoche, also known as corn smut or Mexican truffle, is a fungus that infects maize kernels, turning them into dark, swollen growths. Despite its appearance, huitlacoche has a savory, earthy flavor reminiscent of mushrooms, making it a popular ingredient in traditional Mexican dishes like quesadillas and soups.

Rocky Mountain Oysters (United States): Rocky Mountain oysters, also known as prairie oysters or calf fries, are deep-fried bull, pig, or sheep testicles. Despite their name, they're not seafood but rather a novelty dish often served at festivals and fairs in the American West. Despite their unusual origins, Rocky Mountain oysters have a mild flavor and tender texture when properly prepared.

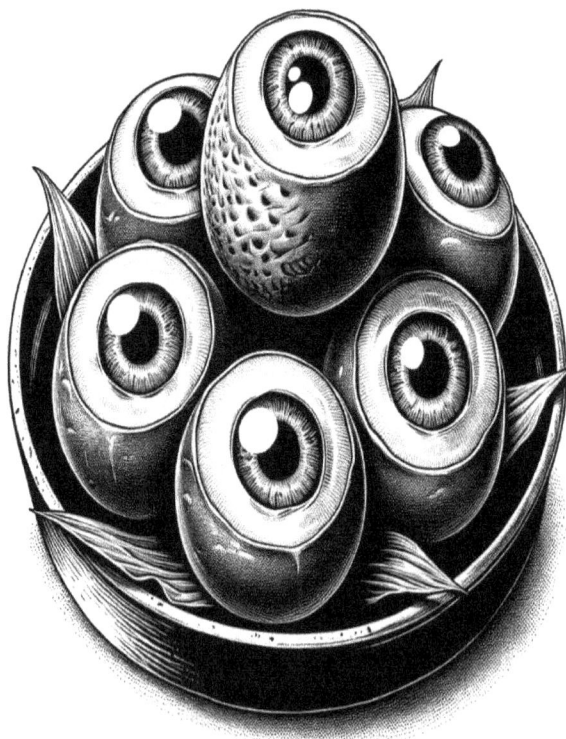

Tuna Eyeballs (Japan)

Tuna eyeballs are a Japanese delicacy often boiled or stewed and prized for their gelatinous texture and rich umami flavor. Despite their appearance, which may be off-putting to some, tuna eyeballs are considered a prized delicacy in Japan and are often enjoyed as a snack or side dish.

Hákarl (Iceland): Hákarl is a traditional Icelandic dish made from fermented shark meat, specifically the Greenland shark, which contains high levels of urea and trimethylamine oxide, making it toxic if consumed fresh. To prepare hákarl, the shark meat is buried underground and left to ferment for several months before being hung to dry for several more, resulting in a strong ammonia smell and a pungent taste. Despite its challenging flavor and odor, hákarl is considered a cultural delicacy in Iceland and is often served as part of a traditional Icelandic feast known as Þorrablót.

Sago Worms (Southeast Asia): Sago worms are the larvae of the red palm weevil and are considered a delicacy in parts of Southeast Asia, including Malaysia and Indonesia. These fat, cream-colored larvae are often found inside the trunk of sago palm trees and are harvested for their high protein content. Sago worms can be eaten raw or cooked, with a taste described as creamy and slightly nutty, making them a popular snack or ingredient in traditional dishes.

Witchetty Grubs (Australia)

Witchetty grubs are the larvae of the cossid wood moth and are considered a traditional Aboriginal bush food in Australia. These white, grub-like larvae are rich in protein and are typically eaten raw or lightly cooked, with a nutty flavor and a texture like scrambled eggs. Despite their appearance, Witchetty grubs are valued for their nutritional content and are often consumed as a delicacy in indigenous Australian communities.

Origins of Language

Bow-Wow Theory: The Bow-Wow Theory suggests that language originated from imitating natural sounds, particularly those made by animals. This theory posits that early humans attempted to mimic the sounds of their environment, such as animal calls, as a means of communication.

Ding-Dong Theory: Contrary to the Bow-Wow Theory, the Ding-Dong Theory proposes that language originated from the instinctive vocalizations humans make in response to physical experiences, such as pain or pleasure. According to this theory, the sounds produced by these experiences evolved into the basis of linguistic expression.

Pooh-Pooh Theory: The Pooh-Pooh Theory proposes that language originated from interjections and exclamations used to express emotions and reactions. This theory suggests that early human communication began with simple vocalizations like "pooh" or "ah" to convey feelings and intentions.

The Mother Tongue Hypothesis: The Mother Tongue Hypothesis suggests that language originated from the bond between mothers and infants, particularly through early forms of babbling and vocal interaction. According to this hypothesis, the nurturing relationship between mother and child played a crucial role in the development of early communication.

The Ta-Ta Theory: The Ta-Ta Theory suggests that language originated from the repetition of simple syllables or sounds, like babbling. This theory posits that early humans gradually expanded their repertoire of vocalizations, leading to the development of more complex linguistic structures.

The Drumbeat Theory: The Drumbeat Theory proposes that language originated from the rhythmic patterns of percussion instruments, such as drums. According to this theory, early humans used drum beats to communicate across distances, conveying messages and coordinating activities within their communities.

The Gesture Theory

The Gesture Theory suggests that language originated from manual gestures and body language, rather than vocalizations. According to this theory, early humans used hand signals, facial expressions, and other forms of non-verbal communication to convey meaning and interact with each other.

The Sing-Song Theory: The Sing-Song Theory proposes that language originated from rhythmic vocalizations, like chanting or singing. According to this theory, early humans used melodic patterns and intonations to communicate emotions, intentions, and social cues.

The Ooga-Booga Theory: The Ooga-Booga Theory suggests that language originated from onomatopoeic expressions, where words mimic the sounds, they represent. According to this theory, early humans used simple, repetitive vocalizations like "ooga" or "booga" to denote objects, actions, and events in their environment.

The La-La Theory: The La-La Theory suggests that language originated from musical expressions, such as singing or chanting. This theory posits that early humans used rhythmic vocalizations to convey meaning and communicate with each other before the development of more structured linguistic forms.

The Yo-He-Ho Theory: The Yo-He-Ho Theory proposes that language originated from the coordinated efforts of early humans engaged in physical tasks, such as hunting or gathering. According to this theory, repetitive vocalizations like "yo," "he," and "ho" were used to synchronize movements and coordinate group activities.

The Cave Art Theory: The Cave Art Theory suggests that language originated from early forms of visual communication, such as cave paintings and symbols. According to this theory, early humans used imagery and symbolic representations to convey meaning and share knowledge with each other.

The Hee-Haw Theory: The Hee-Haw Theory proposes that language originated from the imitation of natural sounds, specifically those produced by non-human primates such as apes and monkeys. According to this theory, early humans may have adapted and modified these primal vocalizations to communicate with each other.

The Tool-Making Theory: The Tool-Making Theory proposes that language originated from the collaborative efforts of early humans engaged in toolmaking and craftsmanship. According to this theory, verbal instructions, expressions, and commands were used to coordinate tasks, share knowledge, and innovate new technologies within prehistoric communities.

The Migration Route Theory

The Migration Route Theory suggests that language originated from the need to communicate during long-distance migrations and travels. According to this theory, early humans developed linguistic systems to coordinate movements, navigate landscapes, and exchange information with other groups encountered along their migration routes.

The Ritual Dance Theory: The Ritual Dance Theory suggests that language originated from rhythmic movements and gestures performed during ceremonial rituals and dances. According to this theory, early humans used choreographed movements and symbolic gestures to communicate religious beliefs, social roles, and cultural traditions within their communities.

The Fire Circle Theory: The Fire Circle Theory proposes that language originated from communal gatherings around fires, where early humans engaged in storytelling, rituals, and social interactions. According to this theory, the shared experiences and oral traditions passed down within these fire circles contributed to the development of language and cultural identity.

The Dream Vision Theory: The Dream Vision Theory suggests that language originated from the interpretation of dreams and visionary experiences. According to this theory, early humans used storytelling and narrative techniques to recount their dreams, share insights, and convey spiritual or supernatural beliefs within their communities.

The Food Sharing Theory: The Food Sharing Theory proposes that language originated from cooperative activities such as food sharing and communal meals. According to this theory, early humans used vocalizations and gestures to coordinate hunting and gathering efforts, distribute resources, and strengthen social bonds within their groups. By sharing information about food sources, coordinating group movements, and establishing social hierarchies, early humans could more effectively ensure their survival and collective well-being. Moreover, communal meals provided opportunities for social bonding and the transmission of cultural knowledge, laying the foundation for the emergence of complex language systems as integral components of human society and culture.

Cryptic Codes and Ciphers

The Dorabella Cipher: The Dorabella Cipher is a cryptogram sent to composer Edward Elgar in 1897 by an unknown correspondent named Dorabella. Despite Elgar's attempts to decipher the message, it remains unsolved to this day, prompting speculation about its meaning and purpose.

The Shugborough Inscription

The Shugborough Inscription is a cryptic message carved into a monument in Staffordshire, England, which has puzzled scholars for centuries. While some believe it holds the key to hidden treasure, others suggest it may be a memorial or an elaborate practical joke.

The D'Agapeyeff Cipher: The D'Agapeyeff Cipher is a cryptographic challenge presented in the book "Codes and Ciphers" by Alexander D'Agapeyeff in 1939. Despite its simplicity, the cipher has remained unsolved for decades, baffling cryptanalysts and amateur codebreakers alike.

The D'Amico Ciphers: The D'Amico Ciphers are a series of cryptograms allegedly created by Italian artist and architect Giovanni Battista D'Amico in the 19th century. Despite claims of their authenticity, the ciphers have been dismissed as hoaxes by many experts, adding to their mystique and intrigue.

The Copiale Cipher: The Copiale Cipher is a cryptogram discovered in a secret society's archives in Germany, dating back to the late 18th century. Deciphered in 2011, the cipher revealed the rituals and symbols of society, shedding light on its secretive practices and organizational structure.

The Beaufort Cipher: The Beaufort Cipher is a variant of the Vigenère cipher, named after its inventor, Sir Francis Beaufort. While less well-known than the Vigenère cipher, the Beaufort Cipher has its own cryptographic properties and historical significance, playing a role in military communications during World War II.

Kryptos Sculpture: The Kryptos Sculpture, located at the CIA headquarters in Langley, Virginia, features a series of encoded messages carved into its surface. While three of the four messages have been deciphered, the fourth remains unsolved, tantalizing cryptographers and sparking speculation about its hidden meaning.

The Unabomber's Manifesto: The Unabomber, also known as Theodore Kaczynski, sent a manifesto to newspapers in the 1990s outlining his anti-technology beliefs and motivations for his bombing campaign. Written in a cryptic style, the manifesto was eventually published with the hope that someone would be able to decipher its hidden messages and identify the author.

The Phaistos Disc

The Phaistos Disc is a mysterious artifact discovered on the island of Crete, dating back to the Minoan civilization. Covered in a spiral pattern of undeciphered symbols, the disc has confounded archaeologists and linguists, with its purpose and meaning remaining enigmatic.

The Voynich Manuscript: The Voynich Manuscript is an ancient book filled with cryptic illustrations and text written in an unknown script. Despite extensive efforts by scholars and codebreakers, the manuscript's meaning and origins remain a mystery, leading to numerous theories ranging from alchemical secrets to extraterrestrial communication.

The Zimmermann Telegram: The Zimmermann Telegram was a secret message sent by the German Empire to Mexico during World War I, proposing a military alliance against the United States. Intercepted and deciphered by British intelligence, the telegram played a significant role in shaping public opinion and ultimately influencing the United States' decision to enter the war.

The Rosicrucian Cipher

The Rosicrucian Cipher is a cryptographic system associated with the Rosicrucian Order, a secretive esoteric society. While the exact origins and purpose of the cipher remain unclear, it has been linked to Rosicrucian literature and symbolism. Its origins are intertwined with the enigmatic teachings and symbols of the Rosicrucian Order, renowned for its arcane wisdom and occult practices. Despite numerous attempts to decipher its intricate patterns and symbols, the true meaning and purpose of the Rosicrucian Cipher continue to elude cryptographers and historians, fueling speculation about its role in safeguarding the secrets of the Rosicrucian brotherhood. Some believe that the cipher holds the key to unlocking hidden knowledge concealed, while others view it as a symbolic representation of the Order's commitment to secrecy. Whatever its significance, the Rosicrucian Cipher remains a tantalizing enigma that continues to captivate the imagination of those drawn to the mysteries of the occult and the esoteric.

The Della Porta Cipher: The Della Porta Cipher is an encryption method described by Italian polymath Giambattista della Porta in the 16th century. While della Porta claimed that his cipher was unbreakable, modern cryptographers have analyzed its structure and attempted to decipher its encoded messages, exploring its historical significance and cryptographic techniques.

The Chaocipher: The Chaocipher is an encryption method developed by John Byrne in the early 20th century, which he claimed was unbreakable. Despite Byrne's assertions, the Chaocipher remained a mystery until it was deciphered in 2010, revealing its intricate mechanism and challenging traditional cryptographic techniques.

The Kamasutra Cipher: The Kamasutra Cipher is a cryptographic system inspired by the ancient Indian text on human sexuality, the Kama Sutra. This playful cipher substitutes erotic positions and intimate acts for letters or symbols, providing a novel and unconventional approach to encryption.

The Beale Ciphers: The Beale Ciphers are a set of three encrypted messages purportedly containing the location of a hidden treasure. While one of the ciphers has been deciphered, the other two remain unsolved, sparking a treasure hunt that has captured the imagination of cryptographers and treasure seekers for over a century.

The Chaocipher: The Chaocipher is an encryption method developed by John Byrne in the early 20th century, which he claimed was unbreakable. Despite Byrne's assertions, the Chaocipher remained a mystery until it was deciphered in 2010, revealing its intricate mechanism and challenging traditional cryptographic techniques.

Great Philosophical Ideas

Solipsism: Solipsism challenges our understanding of reality by positing that only one's mind can be truly known to exist, while the external world and other minds may be illusions. This philosophical stance underscores the difficulty of confirming the existence of anything beyond one's own subjective experiences and perceptions.

The Simulation Hypothesis

The Simulation Hypothesis suggests that our perceived reality could be a highly advanced computer simulation. This idea, popularized by philosopher Nick Bostrom, raises profound questions about the nature of consciousness, the existence of higher beings and the possibility of multiple layers of simulated realities.

The Allegory of the Cave: Plato's Allegory of the Cave is a powerful metaphor for the journey of enlightenment and the pursuit of knowledge. It prompts us to consider the limitations of our perceptions and the transformative power of philosophical inquiry in transcending ignorance and embracing truth.

The Absurd: Existentialist philosophers like Albert Camus explored the concept of the absurd, highlighting the inherent conflict between humanity's quest for meaning and the indifference of the universe. Camus suggests that embracing the absurdity of existence can lead to a profound sense of freedom and authenticity in the face of life's inherent absurdities.

The Veil of Ignorance: John Rawls' Veil of Ignorance is a thought experiment aimed at designing a just society from a position of impartiality. By suspending knowledge of one's own social status, individuals can create principles of justice that are fair and unbiased, promoting equality and fairness for all members of society.

Eternal Recurrence: Nietzsche's concept of eternal recurrence challenges individuals to live their lives as if they would repeat infinitely. This idea encourages us to confront the inevitability of our actions and decisions, emphasizing the importance of living authentically and embracing life's challenges with courage and affirmation.

The Ship of Theseus: The Ship of Theseus paradox prompts us to consider the nature of identity and change. As the components of a ship are gradually replaced over time, we must grapple with the question of whether it remains the same entity, raising broader philosophical inquiries into personal identity and continuity.

Nominalism vs. Realism: The debate between nominalism and realism delves into fundamental questions about the nature of abstract concepts and universals. Nominalists argue that these concepts exist only as linguistic conventions, while realists posit their objective existence independent of human thought, leading to profound implications for metaphysics and epistemology.

The Trolley Problem: The Trolley Problem presents a moral dilemma that challenges our intuitions about the value of individual lives and the principle of utilitarianism. By forcing individuals to weigh the consequences of their actions, this thought experiment raises complex ethical questions about the nature of moral responsibility and the greater good.

The Omphalos Hypothesis: The Omphalos Hypothesis proposes that the universe was created with the appearance of age, including geological formations and historical events. This idea confronts us with the philosophical implications of apparent evidence and raises questions about the nature of belief, evidence, and divine intervention.

The Problem of Evil: The Problem of Evil calls into question the compatibility of a benevolent and omnipotent deity with the existence of suffering and evil in the world. Philosophers and theologians have grappled with this dilemma for centuries, exploring theological responses and reassessing traditional notions of divine attributes.

The Doctrine of Double Effect: The Doctrine of Double Effect addresses moral dilemmas involving actions with both good and bad consequences. By distinguishing between intended and foreseen effects, this principle guides ethical decision-making and raises questions about the morality of actions with potentially harmful consequences.

The Nature of Beauty: Philosophical discussions of beauty delve into subjective and objective conceptions of aesthetic value, cultural influences on perceptions of beauty, and the relationship between beauty and truth. These inquiries invite us to reflect on the nature of art, aesthetics, and the human experience of beauty in the world.

The Veil of Maya

In Hindu philosophy, the concept of the Veil of Maya represents the deceptive nature of the physical world, which obscures the underlying reality of spiritual truth. It suggests that our perception of reality is often clouded by illusion and sensory experiences, leading to attachment, suffering, and a false sense of separateness. Through spiritual practices such as meditation, self-inquiry, and devotion, individuals strive to pierce through this veil of ignorance and attain a deeper understanding of the true nature of existence. Ultimately, the goal is to transcend the illusions of Maya, attain self-realization, and recognize the inherent unity that connects all beings with the divine source.

The Infinite Regression Problem: The Infinite Regression Problem arises when attempting to provide explanations that require an infinite chain of prior causes or justifications. This philosophical challenge prompts us to consider the limits of explanation and the nature of ultimate truths, raising questions about the possibility of infinite regress and foundational knowledge.

Panpsychism: Panpsychism suggests that consciousness is a fundamental aspect of the universe, present in all matter and energy. This idea challenges conventional views of consciousness as solely a product of complex neural systems, inviting us to reconsider the nature of mind, matter, and the cosmos.

The Absence of Free Will: Philosophical determinism challenges our belief in free will by suggesting that all events, including human actions and choices, are determined by preceding causes and natural laws. This idea prompts us to reconsider our notions of personal agency, moral responsibility, and the nature of causation in the universe.

The Philosophy of Time: Philosophical inquiries into the nature of time explore its subjective experience, flow, and relationship to human perception. Concepts such as eternalism and presentism offer competing explanations for the nature of time, challenging our intuitions about the passage of time and the reality of temporal events.

The Liar Paradox: The Liar Paradox highlights the inherent contradictions that arise when a statement asserts its own falsity. This logical puzzle challenges our understanding of truth and logical consistency, prompting deeper inquiries into the nature of language, logic, and self-reference.

The Multiverse Theory:

The Multiverse Theory suggests that our universe may be just one of countless others, each existing simultaneously but operating under different rules and conditions. This concept stems from the idea that the universe is vast and potentially infinite, allowing for the existence of diverse realms beyond our own. While the Multiverse Theory remains speculative, it has captured the imagination of physicists and cosmologists, prompting exploration into the possibility of alternate realities and the potential implications for our understanding of existence. This theory has led to fascinating discussions about the nature of reality, the origin of the cosmos, and the fundamental principles that govern the universe as we know it.

Famous Trials and Legal Cases

The Salem Witch Trials: In 1692, the Massachusetts Bay Colony was gripped by hysteria and paranoia during the Salem Witch Trials, where over 200 people were accused of witchcraft, resulting in the execution of 20 individuals and the imprisonment of many others. The trials highlighted the dangers of mass hysteria, religious extremism, and social scapegoating, leaving a dark stain on America's colonial history and inspiring cautionary tales about the perils of unjust persecution.

The Nuremberg Trials: The Nuremberg Trials of 1945-1946 brought Nazi war criminals to justice for their roles in the Holocaust and other atrocities committed during World War II. These landmark trials established principles of international law, including the prosecution of individuals for crimes against humanity and the concept of "following orders" not absolving individuals of responsibility for war crimes, setting a precedent for future international tribunals.

The Trial of the Toaster: In 1954, the United States saw the bizarre case of "United States v. Ninety-Five Barrels, More or Less, Alleged Apple Cider Vinegar," where the prosecution sought to prove that the contents of 95 barrels labeled as apple cider vinegar were, in fact, unfit for consumption and mislabeled. This unusual trial showcased the lengths to which authorities would go to ensure consumer protection and the accuracy of product labeling.

The Monkey Trial: The Scopes Trial of 1925, also known as the "Monkey Trial," centered around the prosecution of high school teacher John Scopes for teaching evolution in violation of Tennessee's Butler Act. The trial captured national attention as it pitted fundamentalism against modernism, with renowned lawyers like Clarence Darrow and William Jennings Bryan facing off in a courtroom battle that highlighted the ongoing debate over the teaching of evolution in public schools.

The Trial of Galileo

In 1633, the Italian astronomer Galileo Galilei was tried by the Roman Catholic Church for heresy after espousing heliocentrism, the idea that the Earth revolves around the Sun, contradicting the geocentric model supported by the Church. Despite his scientific discoveries, Galileo was found guilty and sentenced to house arrest, highlighting the tensions between faith and reason during the Scientific Revolution.

The Case of the Tarnished Twenties: In the 1920s, the United States witnessed a series of high-profile trials known as the "Tarnished Twenties," involving scandals ranging from corruption and bootlegging to murder and kidnapping. These trials, including those of Fatty Arbuckle, Sacco and Vanzetti, and Leopold and Loeb, captivated the public's imagination and reflected the societal tensions and moral ambiguities of the Roaring Twenties.

The Trial of the Century: The O.J. Simpson murder trial of 1995, often dubbed the "Trial of the Century," captivated audiences worldwide as former football star O.J. Simpson stood accused of the murders of his ex-wife, Nicole Brown Simpson, and her friend, Ron Goldman. The trial became a media spectacle, marked by sensational revelations, celebrity involvement, and intense scrutiny of the criminal justice system, ultimately resulting in Simpson's acquittal but leaving lingering questions and controversy in its wake.

The Trial of Joan of Arc: In 1431, Joan of Arc, a peasant girl who claimed divine visions and led the French army to victory against the English during the Hundred Years' War, was tried for heresy and witchcraft by an ecclesiastical court in Rouen, France. Despite her courageous defense and steadfast faith, Joan was ultimately convicted and burned at the stake, only to be posthumously exonerated and canonized as a saint centuries later, underscoring the complexities of faith, politics, and justice in medieval Europe.

The Pink Snobbery Trial: In 1887, British socialite Lady Whistledown sued the London Times for defamation after the newspaper referred to her as a "pink snob" in a scathing editorial. The sensational trial, marked by gossip, scandal, and courtroom theatrics, captured the public's imagination and highlighted the power struggles and social dynamics of Victorian high society.

The Trial of the Chicago Seven: In 1969, seven anti-war activists were charged with conspiracy and inciting riots during the 1968 Democratic National Convention in Chicago, leading to a highly contentious and politicized trial that reflected the social upheaval and divisions of the era. The trial, marked by clashes between defendants and presiding judge Julius Hoffman, became a symbol of government repression and the growing resistance to the Vietnam

War, ultimately resulting in acquittals and convictions that were later overturned on appeal.

The Trial of Lizzie Borden

The Lizzie Borden case remains one of the most infamous unsolved murder mysteries in American history, captivating the public's imagination for over a century. Despite the lack of physical evidence linking her to the crimes, Borden's strange behavior and contradictory statements during the investigation fueled suspicion. The case also highlighted societal attitudes towards gender and class, with many people unable to conceive of a young, upper-class woman committing such a brutal crime. To this day, the identity of the perpetrator(s) behind the axe murders of Andrew and Abby Borden remains a subject of speculation and fascination, with numerous theories proposed but no definitive answers.

The Trial of Socrates: In 399 BCE, the Athenian philosopher Socrates was tried and sentenced to death by an Athenian jury on charges of impiety and corrupting the youth of Athens. Socrates' trial and execution, as recounted by his student Plato in the dialogues "Apology" and "Phaedo," have become iconic symbols of the tension between individual conscience and the authority of the state in Western philosophy and jurisprudence.

The McMartin Preschool Trial: The McMartin Preschool trial, one of the longest and most expensive criminal trials in U.S. history, centered around allegations of child abuse and satanic rituals at the McMartin Preschool in California. Despite widespread media coverage and a six-year trial, no convictions were secured, casting doubt on the reliability of the children's testimonies and raising questions about the reliability of recovered memories in criminal investigations.

The Witch Trials of Lindheim: In 1671, the small German village of Lindheim was consumed by hysteria and accusations of witchcraft, leading to the execution of 15 women and men accused of consorting with the devil and practicing black magic. The trials, fueled by religious fervor and social tensions, left a lasting scar on the community, and served as a tragic reminder of the dangers of superstition and persecution.

The Trial of the Scottsboro Boys: In 1931, nine African American teenagers known as the Scottsboro Boys were falsely accused of raping two white women on a train in Alabama, leading to a series of highly publicized trials that exposed the racism and injustice of the American legal system. Despite evidence of perjury and coerced testimony, the Scottsboro Boys faced all-white juries and received harsh sentences, highlighting the systemic racism and endemic prejudice of the Jim Crow era

The Black Sox Scandal: In 1919, members of the Chicago White Sox baseball team were accused of intentionally losing the World Series in exchange for bribes from gamblers, in what became known as the "Black Sox Scandal." The ensuing trial revealed widespread corruption in professional baseball and tarnished the reputation of the sport, leading to the lifetime banishment of eight players, including the legendary "Shoeless" Joe Jackson, and prompting reforms to restore public confidence in America's pastime.

The Trial of the Knights Templar

In the early 14th century, the Knights Templar, a powerful and wealthy medieval Christian order, faced accusations of heresy, blasphemy, and other crimes by King Philip IV of France, leading to their arrest, interrogation, and eventual suppression by the Catholic Church. The Templars' trial and dissolution marked the end of an era of crusading knights and fueled enduring legends and conspiracy theories surrounding their alleged hidden treasures and occult practices.

The Trial of Adolf Eichmann: In 1961, former Nazi SS officer Adolf Eichmann stood trial in Israel for his role in orchestrating the

Holocaust, including the deportation and extermination of millions of Jews during World War II. Eichmann's trial, the first televised trial in history, brought the horrors of the Holocaust to international attention and underscored the importance of prosecuting war criminals and holding them accountable for their crimes against humanity.

The Trial of Jack Ruby: Following his televised shooting of Lee Harvey Oswald, the accused assassin of President John F. Kennedy, nightclub owner Jack Ruby was tried and convicted of murder in a trial marked by intense media scrutiny and conspiracy theories. Ruby's sudden death from cancer while awaiting retrial raised suspicions of foul play and fueled speculation about his motives and possible connections to the JFK assassination.

The Trial of Mata Hari: In 1917, the Dutch exotic dancer and alleged spy Mata Hari was tried and executed by firing squad by the French government on charges of espionage during World War I. Mata Hari's trial captivated the public's imagination with its salacious details and allegations of double-dealing, but her guilt remains a subject of debate among historians, with some suggesting she was a scapegoat for French military failures.

www.ingramcontent.com/pod-product-compliance
Lightning Source LLC
Chambersburg PA
CBHW052110020426
42335CB00021B/2703